This edition, issued in 1955, is for members of The Companion Book Club, 8 Long Acre, London, W.C.2, from which address particulars of membership may be obtained. The book is published by arrangement with the original publishers, Cassell & Co. Ltd.

JUMP FOR JOY

"A blessed companion is a book"—JERROLD

JUMP FOR JOY

*

PAT SMYTHE

THE COMPANION BOOK CLUB
LONDON

Made and printed in Great Britain
for The Companion Book Club (Odhams Press Ltd.)
by Odhams (Watford) Limited
Watford, Herts
S.1155.ZV

FOREWORD

By Lieut.-Col. M. P. Ansell, c.b.e., d.s.o.

It is said that all Englishmen are born horsemen, and yet there are few sayings less true. Englishmen are certainly fortunate in that they have been blessed with a country in which they can enjoy this pursuit, and further, have inherited a love of horses. It can truly be said that many an Englishman is born with the opportunity to become a great horseman, but without work he will never succeed.

I feel honoured to have been invited to write the Foreword to this book—for Pat Smythe, having been given the chance to become a great horsewoman, has succeeded. She reminds me of the good and faithful servant who, in the parable, was given five talents, and by hard work doubled this gift, whereas the lazy steward with one talent buried it and did not take advantage of his opportunities.

To succeed as a horseman one must have a love and understanding of the animal, one must study the horse's character, and perfect sympathy must exist between horse and rider.

I have known Pat for many years, and have always regarded her as a great rider, perhaps one of the greatest, for year after year she has come to the fore with new horses all trained by herself: Finality, Carmena, Leona,

7

Prince Hal, and Tosca. With the help of her mother she had to buy young, unmade horses, and train them from the beginning, and surely, if one succeeds, this must be the proof of a great horsewoman.

This book is not a treatise on the training of the horse, but one vital factor will loom large, the necessity for the love and understanding of the character of each individual horse. Pat has always loved her horses, and I well remember her sadness at the selling of Finality, not because she had said good-bye to a successful animal, but because she had said good-bye to a companion. I have never heard her blame a horse for a mistake, but instead she has always endeavoured to find some reason to forgive the animal. This very sincere sympathy and understanding between Pat and her friends has meant success.

At an important show recently, Pat had won the three major events. I went round to congratulate her; she was sitting on the tail-board of her horsebox drinking tea from a flask, celebrating with Tosca and Prince Hal. There was to be no journey in a luxurious car, for she would drive her companions home in the horsebox.

Pat Smythe has travelled abroad with many of our International Teams. Whatever her fortunes in the jumping ring, she has never failed to spread goodwill. She has done much for this country with her many successes, but I believe she has done even more by the making of friends throughout the world, and accepting her success with all simplicity.

CONTENTS

ILLUSTRATIONS

11

CHAPTER I

IN THE BEGINNING ... BUBBLES

My MOTHER's inspiration came suddenly at teatime one autumn afternoon on the day of my dancing class. "I know," she cried. "It's the ballet that does it—the dancing turns her toes out!" She was right.

And that was the end of my artist career. I was four years old; for about a year I had been riding my brother's pony, Bubbles, and it had long been a family joke that my toes turned atrociously outwards, almost at a right angle to the horse.

Although, with the complacency of all little girls who dance, I was enjoying the new and self-conscious effects of the arabesques I performed in the drawing-room, it was no great hardship to give up my ballet lessons. Three weeks later, in Richmond Park, my toes were seen to be scrupulously correct for riding; and the friendship of Bubbles, combined with the adventurous charm of canters in the park, became the chief pleasures of my four-year-old days around the small house at East Sheen where I had been born on the Thursday morning of 22 November, 1928.

My mother, who died when I was twenty-three, was perhaps the most vivacious personality I have ever known, or ever will know. The daughter of a rural clergyman, she had roamed the countryside of Gloucestershire with three lively older brothers, learned to work the farm animals, often rode wild unbroken horses from Ireland, and would try her hand riding any of them, with or without a saddle.

It was not surprising that Captain Eric Hamilton Smythe, a young, athletic, much-decorated army officer back from the battlefields of Flanders, was captured by Mother's courage and gaiety. They met at a family wedding where Father was best man and Mother a bridesmaid; and they met thereafter as often as Captain Smythe could contrive.

Mother was always the brightest, gayest, and most energetic spirit of any youthful group. My father was always quietly humorous, cautious, and immensely considerate, with a great fund of intelligence and courage. They were perfectly matched when they began life together in a pleasant little house on a new estate in East Sheen within easy reach of my father's office at Babcock & Wilcox, the well-known firm of engineers.

The early years of their marriage were saddened by the loss of their first son, Dicky, from pneumonia at the age of four. However, there was Ronald my brother, and I was the third. My mother was then twenty-four.

I was a troublesome baby it seems because I was always wandering, not only crawling from the nursery into the other rooms and clambering downstairs, but even invading the garden, where I was once discovered on the lawn with a large loaf of bread. Worse followed, for one morning our Nanny encountered Mother on the stairs. "Where's Pat? I thought she was with you," asked Mother anxiously. "I thought you had her," exclaimed Nanny. Soon the search was on, but without success. Her heart in her mouth, Mother dashed into the garden and found the gate unlatched. In the street there was no sign of her two-year-old. She ran down to the corner of the main Upper Richmond Road, but I was not to be seen. Almost in despair she raced on when, crossing another road, she was hailed by a butcher's boy on his cycle, who cried, "Is this your baby, Miss?" and lifted me out of his basket. The meat was duly handed over and received with thanks.

Some months later, however, wanderlust had given place to a somewhat odd form of flat-racing performed in the safety of the garden. Ronald, then six, would help me into a sack, climb into one of his own, and we would race the length of the lawn. The sacks were boldly stencilled with the trademark "Eclipse", and before long our garden races were known throughout the neighbourhood as the Eclipse Stakes. At all events they served my athletic needs until Mother bought, cheaply, the pony we called Bubbles, on which Ronald and I were taught to ride.

Taught is perhaps a misleading term, for I cannot recall ever receiving a "lesson" in the orthodox sense. I was more or less dropped on to Bubbles' back—without stirrups, and with a sheepskin for a saddle. Mother, firmly holding a leading rein, would take me into Richmond Park—her own mount a polo pony called Ñata.

At four, I wondered if ever I would be able to ride without grasping sheepskin or pony's mane with both hands, but I did not have to wait long before a hair-raising runaway adventure miraculously built up my confidence. It happened on a crisp afternoon in early spring, when Mother on Ñata and I on Bubbles were trotting sunnily through the Park. Ñata had been a difficult horse to break in; she had bucked and kicked like a Wild West pony, and only with great patience had Mother succeeded in training her. Suddenly, during our saunter through the Park, a loud yell from a party of picknickers startled Ñata into a frenzy of bucking that almost sent Mother over the pony's head. With her usual skill she kept her seat, but lost her grip on my leading rein, and Bubbles, equally scared, jumped sideways, tossed his head and galloped away—with me, somehow, still on his back.

It was a long, strange ride, twisting and turning through the Park, and although I remember the fear that filled me as Bubbles raced homeward, I remember also the exhilaration and my sensible but quite pointless repetition of "Whoa, Bubbles, whoa!" At any rate, Bubbles and I did not part company, although he galloped through the Park, dragging the leading rein, before heading for the farm where the ponies were stabled. Mother, meanwhile, had managed to calm the frightened Ñata, and hurried back to the farm, terrified; for one thing, she was convinced that the mad dash would break my nerve even if I escaped unhurt; for another, she feared the worst and expected to find my body in the yard even if I succeeded in reaching the stables. To enter the yard involved a sharp turn, on hard concrete, and it seemed impossible that Bubbles and I might negotiate it without tragedy.

All her imagined horrors ended as soon as she reached the stable door. There was Bubbles, as quiet as any seaside donkey—and there was I, still astride him, murmuring: "Nice Bubbles, now I can gallop you all by myself."

Looking back, I reflect that a babe on horseback may often enjoy the charmed safety of a reeling "drunk" in a city street, missing death by a hair's breadth, and with the same innocence of the danger involved. My runaway Richmond ride, far from unnerving me, was like a tonic to my small confidence.

Mother, too, had her escapades with horses. About this time, one of our close friends was the celebrated Johnny Traill, the international polo player, who maintained a thriving *estancia* in the Argentine, and once a year would send over a shipload of ponies to England, to break in and "school" for polo riding.

It became Mother's joyful task to break them in—at Richmond Park, where a few years later I, too, was allowed to ride the polo ponies.

Mother worked hard at the job of dealing with those wild little pampas horses, and usually impressed and pleased Johnny by her ability. One day, out riding, Johnny shouted: "Say, Monica, shall I lasso you?" As he spoke he reined and threw the rope with amazing skill; it sang through the air and settled neatly across Mother's shoulders, pinning her arms to her side. Johnny at once dropped his lasso and cantered across to set her free. But before he could reach her side, the trailing lasso suddenly became caught under her pony's tail. Down lashed the tail and off he bolted, Mother in the saddle with arms pinioned. Strollers in the Park screamed as they leapt out of the way, for the pony was heading straight for the road where two cars were converging. Then, almost at the verge of the grass, the pony stopped, bucked wildly, and threw Mother a yard into the air. She landed, perpendicular, on her head, at the sight of which Johnny was certain she had been killed outright. Quickly he caught the horse before it could wreak further havoc, and returned in fear to the spot where Mother lay prostrate. As he bent over she opened her eyes and smiled, rose a trifle hazily to her knees, and insisted on riding back to the stables. She was plainly "out" on her feet, but the incredible fact of the drama was that her sole injuries turned out to be a dislocated thumb and a bruised stiff neck.

Johnny, thankful she was alive, resolved never again to display the art of lassoing on horseback. Mother's chief concern was that she should make a complete recovery before my father returned home from a business trip in the North, for she knew that he was never happy about her antics with what he called "dangerous" young horses. As things turned out, yet more excitement was to come, for Father himself was to report the story of a narrow escape. After the war, he had become an executive director with a leading London firm of engineers, and during the week of Mother's accident was visiting a new industrial plant in Newcastle. His last words before leaving were: "You're not to ride any of those wilder ponies."

Confined to bed after her fall, Mother was in a cold sweat awaiting his return that night. But Father did not appear, and at midnight an alarming message arrived saying that there had been "an accident at the works", though Father was safe. The accident, we learned, was an explosion which occurred ninety seconds after he had left the factory, and this tragedy delayed Father's homecoming by another week. The respite, along with several osteopathic treatments, gave Mother a chance to recuperate, but she was still clearly an invalid when Father returned.

"What happened to your neck?" he asked, as he sat by her bed.

"I wrenched it getting out of the car," said Mother without a blush.

"And how did you break your thumb?" asked Father.

"It got jammed in the garage door," said Mother, guilelessly.

The pretence was all too much for Father, who broke into a loud laugh as he forcibly expressed his disbelief; but he was never to learn how near to catastrophe she had truly come.

Not that Father was a killjoy—this periodic concern for his wife's safety was as often as not justified. He was as great a lover of sport and physical prowess as Mother, and was a fine golfer, tennis player, and mountaineer. His own father had contracted tuberculosis and gone to live in Switzerland, where the young Eric and his brother were brought up and educated. Father, who spoke fluent French and German, went to school at Lausanne, and later to the University of Heidelberg. His leisure was claimed by the mountains, and even in his teens his name began to mean something to the world of climbers; as a youngster he achieved the distinction of being among the first men to climb the Matterhorn, solo.

Father was impatient for action when the First World War got under way; he had joined the Honourable Artillery Company, and later became a dispatch rider in the Fourth Army division, to which the young Prince of Wales was attached.

He soon got his wish for front-line activity, and before the war was over had been recommended for the D.S.O., won the M.C. and Bar, the Legion d'honneur, and several mentions in dispatches. Oddly enough, his most memorable war experience—or at least the only event he would describe in detail—was the Armistice of 1918. He was in fact the first British officer across the line, for he had been sent to meet the German emissaries and conduct them into the British sector for the historic signing of the Armistice on that solemn November day. "It was a strange moment," he would say, "when I walked off to meet the Germans; and stranger still to shake them by the hand and then lead their defeated officers across the line to finish the war, formally and on paper."

Earlier, Father had been seconded for duties which brought him into close contact with the Prince of Wales. As a liaison officer, he had among other tasks the responsibility of keeping King George V regularly informed of the progress and activities of the young Prince.

More than thirty years later I was to sit at a restaurant table in Montmartre, recalling stories of my father in the days before I was born, with that same Prince and his wife—who had become Duke and Duchess of Windsor.

Father was an excellent horseman, too, although business pressures deprived him of much opportunity for riding; but on fine days we would go—Mother, Ronald and I, and Father whenever he was free—for picnic rides in Richmond Park. While tea was prepared and eaten, the horses would be hobbled—a practice no longer permitted in the Park; and life took on a peaceful rural colour which was altogether surprising for a *ménage* less than half-an-hour's drive from the centre of London. Mother would talk (a shade wistfully, for we were far from wealthy) of her hope that one day soon I would have a pony of my own. Father would tell me, with great good humour, that like all the best horses or cows I came from a line-bred family.

The disturbances in Europe and the unsettled affairs of this country did not touch my happy days at home. Richmond Park was our great playground, we had wonderful games, scouting in the bracken, enjoying the bright colours of the plantations and the rhododendrons, and watching the deer grazing round the Pen Ponds below White Lodge. We would see the young stags rubbing the velvet off their antlers or run away from their violent bellowing in the mating season. I loved the rides through the Park and often wondered what it would be like to jump the Park benches or even to appear in a real horse show on Bubbles like Ronald.

What a day that had been, with Ronald the youngest competitor in the Show. In those years the fashion for children to show ponies was still comparatively novel (to-day they strap babies of ten months to their mounts). Now, here was my brother a prize-winner. It was I who led him from the ring, blinking as the photographers flashed their cameras at us. Next day, Ronald and I, with Bubbles, made the picture page of no less than *The Times,* a publicity achievement which neither of us quite appreciated.

There were also deeper personal factors which drew my thoughts ever closer to horses and ponies. Shortly before my fifth birthday, I caught diphtheria and was at once consigned to an isolation hospital in the country. It was my first separation from Mother and home, and it lasted for ten weeks. I gazed out of my sickroom window and tried to count the sheep on the Mendip hills; then the sight of a half-dozen ponies set me thinking that a horse's life must be lonely without a rider, and soon I began fretting over the loneliness of Bubbles and the polo ponies at home, mistaking their needs, doubtless, for what was undoubtedly my own longing for familiar family surroundings. Eventually, after what seemed like a year of absence, I was brought home and greeted with huge affection. I found I had to learn to walk again.

Occasionally, the next year, we were taken to Roehampton, to swim and to watch the polo. By the time I was five, I was known to all who watched my bathing antics as the Floating Smile. It seemed that my breast-stroke resembled the movements of a frog more accurately than any child had ever before achieved, aside from which I would swim with head far out of the water and a wide, bland, unconscious grin on my face. Ronald and I were almost as good at swimming under water as on top, but for some reason I was exceptionally fearful about attempting to dive, although out of the water I could perform expert handstands. I would hover on the edge of the pool for a full half-hour, striving for courage. One day Ronald gaily suggested that the best way to dive was first to make a handstand on the edge of the springboard, and then to fall head-first into the water. He promised sixpence if I succeeded. I accepted the challenge, but still could not bring myself to the point of execution. But, after long hesitation and countless retreats, I managed the handstand, flopped into the water and emerged, choking but triumphant.

Ronald sauntered off, refusing to pay up, because, he said, "You took far too long about it." I am not sure that I have ever wholly forgiven him for the treachery.

CHAPTER 2

KING, PAGE, AND PIXIE

MY BROTHER Ronald dominated me in an exceedingly pleasant fashion, despite the incident at the swimming pool. For seven years we preserved a fantasy relationship of "King and Page", in which I was the servile but far from downtrodden subject. Ronald's sovereignty, dictatorial though never oppressive, expressed itself mostly in terms of "Fetch me yonder ball, page," or "Carry this message to the castle, page." If I served him well I was rewarded by promotion to the rank of Lieutenant or Captain. But great was my dread lest the reverse should happen and I was demoted—perhaps to 3rd Class Page!

But we were saved, perhaps, from the worst effects of elder-brother domination by two things: the first was that I responded willingly and with huge energy to every activity born out of Ronald's unusually inventive imagination; the second was that before long I achieved a healthy superiority of my own in everything concerning horses.

In the summer of 1935 my brother and I were taken to Town for the Silver Jubilee of King George V and Queen Mary. The day of that royal drive through London was hot and sunny, and at one stage a shade too overpowering even for the King; as the open carriage passed us, Queen Mary somewhat unceremoniously nudged her husband, who seemed to have dozed off in the heat—he awoke with a start, whereupon the crowd smiled and doubly cheered their affection.

The horses in the great procession pushed me one step further towards acquiring a pony of my own; we all had seats and a fine view of the royal pageant on its route, and much of my admiration went to the superbly-trained horses of the Royal Mews. I did not realize that Mother and Father had already decided that they would find me a pony before the summer was out. A week or two later we set off on a holiday-tour of Somerset and Devon, our declared purpose "to find a pony for Pat".

Down to the New Forest and over to Somerset, through the Devon villages and over to Dartmoor, with Ronald, Mother, and Father in fine form, keeping me in laughter until I ached. Among the charades as we bowled along, the most uproarious was a game called "Mr. Quigley's Caravan", with our family four-seater in the leading rôle. No vehicle ever displayed such eccentric habits or suffered odder mishaps. "Stop! Stop," my father would shout in sudden alarm. "What on earth has happened, dear Mr. Quigley?" Mother would cry. "Calamity! The roof of the caravan has blown away—and the rain is pouring in!" Ronald would shout more in joy than sorrow. Sometimes it was the roof, sometimes the wheels would drop right off, or the walls would collapse; there were dozens of similar idiocies, and I was always completely helpless with laughter. It was a happy, memorable, boisterous journey *en famille*—and that was something I was not often to enjoy.

We saw ponies by the hundred, and for me the impatience to choose one was constantly tempered by the wish that our happy family drive could last for ever. But then, in the Dartmoor country, we came upon her —the pony of my daydreams. She was a handsome chestnut mare, about thirteen hands, a spirited five-year-old with a substantial will of her own and an immense sense of fun. Her mother was a Dartmoor pony, her father an Arab, and she had been bred on the Prince of Wales's farm at Tor Royal.

From the moment we saw her I wanted her for my own, and there seemed little more for life to offer when Mother and Father cheerfully announced that we would buy her at once and bring her home to Richmond. I cannot now remember whose flash of genius it was, but she was given a name that suited her perfectly. We called her Pixie; and she was *my* pony.

In the months that followed I took some hard knocks and falls, and indeed have never since been bucked off as often as I was with Pixie. Yet we soon established a deep if prosaic friendship, even if it mostly took the form of a battle of wills. I would exercise her on the polo field at Ham Common, where she would canter about a hundred yards and then become bored; so she would buck me off and proceed to gallop around the field, bucking hard like a pony in a rodeo. Then she would pause, gaze about her to establish my whereabouts, canter in a straight line towards me and finally come to a standstill with an air of mock meekness. Then I would climb aboard again and she would go through the same comedy, always coming back to me with a gentle invitation to try another ride. One day, in the middle of Richmond Park, I succeeded in fooling Pixie by leaping off before she could begin her bucking; but it made no difference, for she gave her stylish rodeo display as usual, and kept it up for so long that scores of cars began lining the roadside, their astonished passengers applauding Pixie's hilarious performance. One man came forward to tell me pompously that I should go to fetch my father. "That horse has obviously been stung by a wasp," he told me with a knowledgeable air. I grinned and tried to explain that Pixie was merely having her fling, but he stalked away muttering that children these days paid no attention to the advice of their elders.

Life suddenly became charged with a great flurry, for about this time Mother and Father decided to move from Shotfield Avenue to a roomier, pleasanter house with a high-walled garden, at the end of a cul-de-sac called Gipsy Lane, near Barnes Common. It was still very much a country existence, and far from neglecting "our" Richmond Park, we merely added the common at Barnes to our places of recreation. Ronald, now a boarder at a boys' preparatory school, came home for holidays. Father travelled here and there on business. Mother was often busy with the housekeeping, but she always found time to encourage my interest in the horses and to take me out riding.

It was then that I began to get a passion for jumping. By the time we had settled into Beaufort, our new house, I had acquired two mice and a white rabbit. In order to reach their meals they had to jump over a series of obstacles constructed in their run. Snow White the rabbit proved an apt pupil and even the mice thrived on this athletic training and managed to produce a large family, ranging in every colour from Tim the ginger one to Tiddler the black and white mother. Best of all was

27

Raider, our cairn terrier. He was the third generation from a cairn bitch given to Mother as a wedding-present. My parents and Raider were equally long-suffering while I barricaded the house so that he had no escape while I was teaching him to jump. It was not long, however, before the maid was able to bring the tea-tray into the drawing-room without the hazard of being confronted by the stepladder on its side across the door, the chairs lying in a line down the passage, and all possible escape routes blocked with cushions, for Raider had soon learnt that the line of least resistance was to leap over any obstacle in front of him. He later got so good that he would jump over a walking stick held quite high or through the curve of my arms or even through my moving bicycle when I put my feet on the handlebars. Then we began to build steeplechase courses for ourselves on the lawn and gallop over the deckchairs until we fell exhausted.

Unfortunately I frequently suffered from nettlerash, and on one of these occasions was kept in bed for several days. Anxious about the animals, for it was always explicitly understood that the responsibility for their feeding and toilet was mine. I asked Mother who would look after them. "Don't worry, I'll ask Mr. Kemp to attend to that," she said (the Kemps were a friendly Cockney couple who cooked and kept house for us). In the middle of my first morning in bed Mr. Kemp, wearing a solemn expression, pushed his head around my door and said: "I'm just going out to feed the rabbits." I thanked him and he disappeared in the direction of the kitchen. A few moments later I watched him cross the garden towards the rabbit hutch; he looked very dignified and unusually formal as he walked the lawn in the manner of a well-trained butler. Balanced on the palm of his left hand was our largest silver tray on which he bore a small china bowl containing bran and cold tea-leaves. Mr. Kemp was clearly enjoying his newest chore.

Gradually my ideas about jumping spread to riding and one day, while the grown-ups were practising polo, I had a sudden impulse to try Pixie over some show-jumps that had just been left in the corner of the field. Neither of us had jumped before, but Pixie in her astonishment leaped high in the air over the first fence at which I put her. I went flying, and the polo game was rudely interrupted by my yells of hurt pride.

Pixie's main trouble was caution, I found. As we approached an obstacle, she would hesitate at the crucial moment before her take-off, and then, nervously, would jump four times higher than the fence—a feat not in the least difficult since Pixie had unusually strong quarters and a phenomenal "spring". Her jumps were often enormous, with the result that I constantly fell off. But in general I suffered more from loss of dignity than from any serious physical hurt, and after several weeks of patient effort found that Pixie was more stable—and so, consequently, was I.

Ronald came home for the holidays to join Mother and me in afternoons of illicit jumping at Richmond; we would jump anything that came our way—park benches, ditches, fallen trees and stiles, a sport kept full of excitement owing to the need for avoiding the park-keepers, for although riding was permitted almost anywhere in Richmond Park back in the thirties, jumping was greatly frowned upon.

During this period we kept Pixie near the Park, on

Ham Common where we had a small paddock, her main sustenance (and she seemed to thrive on it) being grass mowings thrown over the fence. Along with my initial jumping experiences with Pixie, I was also riding the Johnny Traill polo ponies which Mother had broken in. Again, with a sheepskin for a saddle, which doubtless helped to give me an extremely secure "seat". Mother showed me, too, the art of schooling a pony into obedience and co-operation, and I was soon performing figures of eight and a dozen other basic exercises. Other people were now bringing their ponies to Mother for schooling, and I would ride them, too. I was somewhat surprised to discover that I could handle a variety of horses with ease, but only later did I realize that it was the superb experience provided by Pixie's peccadilloes that made this possible.

My first competitive appearance in public was, to say the least, a flop.

Soon after my eighth birthday I joined the pony club of the Mid-Surrey Drag Hunt, which involved a lengthy hack through the southern suburbs to reach the rallies which were held around Epsom or Leatherhead. Ronald and I would take it in turns to ride Pixie (we had long ago grown out of the gentle Bubbles), while Mother would drive down in the car. I was overjoyed on the day I learned that I would be allowed, at last, to take part in the pony club hunter trials. It was my week-end début in competition, and it did not occur to me that it could end ingloriously. One of the contests turned out to be "jumping in threes", and my cup was full, so to speak, when two girls slightly older than I asked if I would care to ride and jump with them.

In the sunshine, a good crowd watched as we lined up for the start—altogether a scene of rural prettiness, with my two companions mounted on bigger ponies, and me in the middle, astride Pixie. With a few seconds to go, a woman's voice drifted across. . . . "How charming the little one looks, don't you think . . . quite, quite charming." Does she mean *me*, I wondered, and the whole world began to glow.

Suddenly we were off, and the first fence loomed ahead. Pixie was going well, and there was a sense of both danger and comfort in the nearness of the pony racing on each side of me, not more than a nose ahead. Now we faced the fence, I steadied for our take-off, and jumped.

The pain was what hit me first, but still more intense was the hurt of the sudden collapse in all my new pride and hope and joy. We had actually collided in mid-air —all three of us. To make matters worse, my two girl companions had staggered on, and recovered their balance, but I was unseated, and poor Pixie landed on her side on top of me. As often happens, we were both uninjured, apart from a shooting pain in my ankle. I scrambled up, caught hold of a slightly confused Pixie, clambered aboard and finished the course, Pixie hanging back most of the way, justifiably nervous about approaching the other two ponies.

When it was all over, I could barely walk; the ankle had swollen alarmingly and a fracture was suspected. Next day, a hospital appointment for an X-ray was made, and, thirty minutes late, I hopped and skipped the last three hundred yards to the out-patients' department, to learn, happily, that a severe sprain was all I had sustained.

But my week-end fiasco served only to strengthen the longing to jump with skill, grace, and power, and Mother's exhortations to remember that I was, after all, just a little girl of eight, seemed no more than the familiar, irritating superiority of "grown-up" advice to the young. I could not know that the slight, golden-haired, attractive Mother who was always so busy and bright, counted my attachment to the horses among her deepest joys, and my success with them among her profoundest hopes for the future.

I did not have to wait long for my next momentous ride, for one month before my ninth birthday, Mother took me again into Surrey for my first taste of hunting, or rather cubbing, with the Surrey Union Hounds. This was a new kind of thrill, not the least enchanting side of which was getting up at four in the morning to drive to Holmwood where the meet was to be held. I had already ridden Pixie down the evening before, and when we arrived at Holmwood for the meet, she greeted me with one of her old displays of rodeo bucking. When she had settled down, I walked her around in the crisp autumn morning before the hunt began. We had a good run that day, and at the end of it I was presented with the brush. I was well and truly "blooded".

At this time I was attending a day school in Wimbledon, thankful to be living at home where all my weekends could be devoted to the ponies, and to training Pixie in a hundred-and-one tricks that would be useful in the gymkhanas for which I was soon to enter. Pixie was an extraordinarily intelligent pony; she learned to shake "hands", allowed me to vault on to her back over her tail, and to perform acrobatics—generally adoring her rôle in athletic games or unusual forms of fun. At Musical Chairs she became expert, and quickly learned that when the music stopped that was the moment to turn and gallop for the chair in the centre of the ring. I entered her for a few small shows and won my first juvenile rosettes, a riding whip, a bridle, and a manicure set which I use to this day. Then, at Ferne Gymkhana, in Dorset, Pixie achieved a 1st, 2nd, and 3rd prize. Among other events, we won the Bob-Apple Race, where I soaked myself in a frantic scramble for the bucket of water. We had our picture in *The Tatler*, and I felt that I had truly "arrived". I was nearly ten.

When I look back on the years before the war I cannot help being immensely grateful for the happiness we had as a family. The school holidays were the best time because we were all together. Ronald and I would ride a good deal—the polo ponies as well as Pixie—but it was quite a long way to the Park, and more often than not we would play games on Barnes Common. Mother was very fond of music and would often play the piano while my father sang Gilbert and Sullivan or German *lieder* in a pleasant baritone. Ronald had Mother's musical gifts and loved to play and compose. Sometimes he organized concerts in which I would recite, sing or play, or we would gather round Mother at the piano yelling Gaudeamus songs or the latest Hill Billies. (He would embellish his stories with musical accompaniments which made them all the more effective. I remember once being reduced to tears by some pathetic musical tale.)

One summer Ronald could not come on holiday with us. My father had a business acquaintance in Paris who offered to take him in exchange with his own son, so in place of my brother we had Jean Montois to live with us and learn English. His first greeting when I opened the door to him was surprising. He took my hand shyly and murmured most politely, "Good-bye". Jean had a delightful sense of humour and was very good company when we all went down to Fordingbridge in the New Forest for our holiday. We fished and walked and rode for hours. Jean was very bad about going to bed, like most Frenchmen I suppose he felt that life began at 8 p.m. I can remember my father chasing Jean round the garden exclaiming in mock severity, "*Au lit, Jean*", and Jean fleeing in simulated terror shouting "*Pas encore, monsieur.*" In London Jean and I used to amuse ourselves running *up* the tube escalators that were coming down. I think he considered that the best part of London: I certainly had no use for the city. In Ronald's absence, however, it was not Jean who won my affection, but a young fisherman on holiday at Fordingbridge. I fell for him completely and he wrote me the most charming letters. He has since become one of the fastest men on record—in an aeroplane.

Some of our best holidays were at Christmas and this was because we used to go down to my uncle and aunt at Swindon Manor near Cheltenham, a charming, rambling old house with a lovely garden. This was my introduction to the Cotswolds which I love so much. My uncle, Col. Gordon Smythe, encouraged every sign of interest we showed in horses and generously helped us in many ways. So excited would I be just before our visits that I frequently ran a temperature and had to be left behind. Next time Mother simply did not tell me that we were spending Christmas at uncle's, and this device seemed to work the required miracle cure.

Somewhat less easy to cure was the arthritis which now increasingly troubled Father, and already there was talk —which he and Mother often conducted in French to combat my curiosity—of his going to France or Switzerland for prolonged treatment; in fact, his departure did not take place until after war had broken out, and at this time—it was, I think, the spring of 1938—we began planning what was to be the last but one of those family holidays I loved so well.

The most memorable of these idyllic pre-war holidays was spent in the Lake District, at the home of an uncle and aunt who lived in the lovely White Moss neighbourhood. The day after our arrival, uncle presented Ronald with an exceedingly smart-looking trout fishing rod, and showed him how to use it. In order that I should not feel neglected I received a rod, too—a somewhat old, worn bamboo type which was doubtless assumed to be adequate for a mere schoolgirl who was unlikely in any event to handle a line successfully. With basket and bucket, lunch packets and rods, Ronald and I set off for a stream near Grasmere, where we settled ourselves for the afternoon. It became an ironic situation for, despite his patience and a variety of baits, Ronald and his gleaming rod were scorned, as if deliberately, by the fish, while my much-despised bamboo rod hauled them in at a maddening rate. Next day, however, the tables were turned. In a small boat we rowed on to the lake to spin for pike, and after an hour or two of spinning we succeeded in catching four. Triumphantly we rowed back to the lakeside, where I placed my pair of pike—now dead, or so I thought—in a bucket and raced off to bring

Mother and Father who were strolling nearby. Excitedly, holding a hand on each side and chattering all the way, I dragged them to the water's edge. There, when we were ten yards away, I watched in horror as my pike, one by one, suddenly made graceful, curving leaps out of my bucket, into the lake.

To soften the disappointment, Mother and Father took us to a secluded, narrow part of the stream for a game which always delighted me, and at which Ronald and both my parents were wonderfully skilled. It consisted of diverting a stream, fashioning a small "lake", and decorating its surroundings in various ingenious ways. That day, they made miniature dams, a series of incredibly beautiful hanging gardens, a mountain, and even a waterfall. I busied myself collecting small plants and pieces of shrub and moss which became the trees of our lakeside, all on the most minute scale. When it was finished we lay on the grass to hear Father re-telling his stories of Switzerland and the satisfactions of mountain climbing. Suddenly I remembered the hint that he might be leaving England, and all at once I felt a strange longing to be with him on the summit of that Matterhorn which he had conquered before I was born.

In the days that followed, Ronald and I would go for long walks into the hills and bathe in the tarns until we were blue with cold. Mother and Father were constantly astounded at our toughness, but since we seemed to thrive on such naked spartan activity they made no protest about our swimming excursions. One afternoon brought an alarming experience. My brother and I still pursued, with great enjoyment, our "King and Page" charade, and as a rule I was a willing-enough servant in return for the adventurous pastimes his vivid imagination created. But on this occasion, while we were resting after a strenuous climb over White Moss, he told me one of his more garish ghost stories. He could tell them brilliantly, with a spine-chilling technique resembling an Edgar Allan Poe tale, and although Mother was often furious with him after I had awakened, screaming, from a nightmare, I loved his stories and would never have wanted him to stop. The epic that he called "The Ghost of White Moss" was a particularly vivid and gruesome effort. Eventually it ended, and we continued our walk. A few minutes later, once more in his rôle of the King, Ronald asked me to return to the house, some twenty minutes' downhill walk, to fetch his mackintosh because the sky was beginning to look threatening.

The journey involved a careful trek through the centre of two stretches of marshland surrounded by trees and scrub, and as I reached the second of these bogs a blackish cloud darkened the sky and it thundered. Suddenly I was filled with terror. Ronald's story returned in all its murkiness, and I was convinced that the Ghost of the Bog would rise from steamy depths to envelop me for ever. Somehow, it all became mixed with *The Hound of the Baskervilles* which I had finished reading over breakfast that morning. I gave a startled jump to see what lay behind me, turned again and made a dash for home, pursued by wild dogs and wilder apparitions. Nevertheless, the fright failed to cure me of my appetite for Ronald's stories, and within a week I was asking for more.

Home again to Beaufort, from where I took Pixie to

the horse show at Ranelagh, where the ground later became a sprawl of allotments. This was the first time I had been faced with a fairly large and critical array of spectators, but any resulting nervousness was as nothing compared with my faster heartbeats at the sight of the large, red brick wall which we would have to jump. I wondered if we would ever get over it without disaster, and I am certain the jump could not have turned out to be the resounding success it was, without the charming, apt, and perfectly-timed verbal encouragement that was shouted by an enterprising Irishman at a crucial moment. I set off to jump my round, but when Pixie came to the red brick wall she stopped, and gave it a close, impudent scrutiny. I flushed slightly in shame, and was about to turn back for a second attempt when the Irish voice said, loudly:

"Hup!"

Pixie at once raised her head, straightened up, and jumped the wall from a standstill. Nobody was more surprised than I.

As a family, our last holiday together, before the war brought the separations which were soon to end the sense of unity we had known for ten years, took place in the summer of 1939. Ronald was now a boarder at Gresham's School, in Norfolk, and it was not far away, at West Runton, that we passed a boisterous fortnight. It was in a sense the most childish of all our holidays, and one which yet marked the end of my childhood. Close to the sea was the summer camp of a noisy but well-disciplined crowd of boys from Dr. Barnardo's Homes, who drilled and trained, as cadets, in the arts of seamanship. We made great friends with the Barnardo boys, and for one in particular—a tousle-haired youth known throughout the camp as Nigger—I had a great admiration, especially when he paraded in his smart sailor uniform (indeed, we corresponded with some seriousness for two years afterwards).

The most popular sport of each day was a crude form of sand-skiing, performed by Ronald, Nigger, a half-dozen other boys from the camp, and me. It was a perilous game—racing headlong at a cliff of soft sand, launching into space and hurtling, with knees bent and arms stretched like wings, some twenty feet below where we landed in a gentler slope of sand on the beach. Ronald was more or less the champion of the gang, and with great courage and some degree of skill he would sail through the air, achieving record distances. More often t'an not, I would hit my chin with my knees.

It was a glorious "fling" of a holiday, despite the fact that it ended in farce and much pain.

We were having a farewell picnic. . . .

On my knees in the sand, I was stretching for a sandwich. At that moment someone jogged someone else's elbow, but unhappily the hand belonging to it held a vacuum flask of scalding tea, and not even the most careful aim could have spilled it more surely across my behind.

Fourteen nights passed before I could sleep on my back . . . and I still possess the scar.

CHAPTER 3

RIDING THROUGH THE WAR

NINETEEN-THIRTY-NINE was the year that the blackout came to Pixie as well as to Europe, although in Pixie's case it was but half a blackout, and unlike Europe it strengthened rather than cramped her style.

The fact is that Pixie went totally blind in one eye, following a powerful kick by another horse—no cloven-hoofed Hitler with a maniacal hatred for chestnut mares, merely an undistinguished pony, schooled on Ham Common, who let fly with his hind legs while Pixie was innocently nibbling tufts of grass. Inconsolable at first, I feared it meant that Pixie would have to die—and I had barely recovered from my first experience of death, when Raider the Cairn had swallowed a sharp-pointed bone and fatally injured himself. My distress faded, however, when I learned that Pixie would recover after several weeks of convalescence, although all the veterinary efforts available would not be able to save her sight.

When, eventually, I saddled, rode, and jumped her again I found an amazing change in her abilities. True, the one-eyed Pixie began going at her fences in a manner not quite so straight and sure as before—but once she reached them, lo and behold, she began jumping higher than ever and with still greater zest. Observing this,

Mother decided on an ambitious step. She entered Pixie and me for the Children's Jumping Class at Richmond Royal Horse Show—in those days the chief function for the *crème de la crème* of show jumping, since there was neither a Harringay nor a White City spectacle. As luck would have it, I caught 'flu, and a few days before the Show was still in bed with a temperature in the hundreds. Mother got me up on the morning of the Show, recovered but still absurdly weak for any form of athletics, and only the vehemence of my protests kept her from sending me at once back to bed. My face white as the sheets I had just left, I rode Pixie from home to the Richmond Show, across Richmond Park, where we jumped a half-dozen benches on the way for practice and limbering up.

As Mother and I reached the large closed gates of the Show, I said: "Is there anything like aspirin, Mummy, to keep your knees from trembling?" At that moment I would cheerfully have taken chloroform, but since neither was forthcoming, into the ring we went.

Within five minutes my one-eyed Pixie had banished every trace of show nerves and post-'flu depression. She jumped more brilliantly than I had ever known and gave me for the first time a sense of what might be achieved by a partnership of true understanding between rider and pony. Pixie, indeed, responded to every touch, and went round—in contest with many fine ponies—performing jump-off after jump-off without so much as scraping the dirt from the fences. Only once was there a familiar moment of hesitation, when we approached a high fence of a type we had never met before. It bore a bold ROAD CLOSED sign. Coming up to it, Pixie stopped dead, turned her sound eye towards the lettering and carefully inspected the sign, nodding at the words as if she were mentally spelling them out. Satisfied that there were no errors, she jumped the fence from a standstill while the crowd gave an approving roar of laughter.

In the end, after jumping four clear rounds and tackling fences which had now, inch by inch, gone up to the Open jumping height, Pixie tied for first place with another pony. It was not a bad victory for a one-eyed chestnut mare with little experience and only an unquenchable spirit to carry her through.

When we got back to Beaufort it was late, Father had come home and retired to bed. He seemed to be in pain as he leaned an elbow on the pillow and voiced his delight at Pixie's success. There was more talk of Switzerland, or France, or Algeria, of "treatment," and of the doctor's opinion, and my excitement subsided as I puzzled again over this ailment, rheumatoid arthritis, whose name I could barely pronounce.

Later that summer, Ronald and I were sent to the Cotswolds to stay with our Uncle Gordon at Swindon Manor. We had Pixie with us and I was finding new thrills of partnership with one of Uncle's polo ponies called Fireworks. But the atmosphere, not only with the family but with everyone we met, was unsettled, and I felt utterly confused with the talk of impending war and the still uncharted activity called Evacuation. Mother had already added the Red Cross to her busy routine; Father's condition was worsening and he was being advised to give up his job in London.

On 3 September, 1939, I was in Tewkesbury Abbey. The vicar himself came to announce the news of war, and I remember a feeling of incongruity at being in the presence of God while a voice spoke of man's conflict and battle to come. A noise made me turn around—and in the pew behind me a middle-aged woman in a floral hat was sobbing. I began to feel much older than when I had entered the church.

Part of my school at Wimbledon had already moved to the Sussex coast, at Seaford, and a few weeks later I left Uncle's peaceful place in the Cotswolds to join my classmates for a winter of schooling by the sea. There was little atmosphere of battle during the months that followed; the South Downs became entirely snow-covered and more beautiful than I have known them since; we went tobogganing and I also learned to play lacrosse. But I was homesick all the time.

A new separation came with the departure of Father for, of all places, North Africa, in the New Year of 1940. He was sent to Biskra, in Algeria, where it was thought that treatment in a warm, sunny climate would improve his now crippling arthritic condition. Mother, who stayed in London carrying on with her Red Cross duties, began to look round for somewhere to park me so that I could continue my education in safety. I had been staying for Christmas with my uncle and aunt at Swindon Manor, and a few days after Father left England I travelled to London on a visit to Mother at her Red Cross headquarters.

She tried hard to paint a glowing picture. "Wouldn't it be lovely to spend part of the summer down at Ferne?" (This was the Duchess of Hamilton's *ménage*, which I was soon to know well.) Mother went on: "And a few more weeks with Uncle—riding the ponies? And then, perhaps, go to the school the Duchess is starting? Wouldn't that be fun?"

Doubtfully, I said yes it would all be fun; but now that Father had gone and Ronald was away at school, the thought of leaving Mother for months on end filled me with misery. That night, while she was on duty, I slept in her bed at the Red Cross centre, and the next afternoon she took me around London in an effort to cheer me up. We went to a musical show, ate an enormous tea and had a late supper, during which my mind half-acknowledged that although I *ought* to be unhappy, I was already feeling much better. Late in the evening we stood and watched the crowds in the blacked-out Piccadilly Circus and bought roasted chestnuts from a stall run by a man in a white top hat which shone in the darkness—and by the time I climbed into bed I was able to view the future without gloom. Next day, Mother took me in a taxi to Victoria, where I caught the train for Seaford. Back to school, but not for long; soon the authorities decided that south coastal towns might prove unsafe in the event of air raids (no one can deny that they were right), and so school life at Seaford broke up in the widespread helter-skelter of re-evacuation.

I was then sent to the tranquil safety of our friends the Mackintoshes and the Drummond-Hays, who lived on the lovely border of Wiltshire and Dorset. Ahead of me was a golden summer, and the war, which in reality was growing daily noisier and nearer, seemed milder and further away.

Ferne was the home of the Duchess of Hamilton, a white-haired and bright-eyed enthusiast for animal welfare and Christian Science, who was now planning a

44

somewhat free-and-easy school for, among others, her grandchildren—the two boys and two girls of her daughter, Lady Jean Mackintosh, whose husband, Chris, was a celebrated Olympic skiing champion. The children were called Sheena and Vora (girls of about my own age), Douglas, and the baby Sharloch. A few miles away at Dennis Farm, Tisbury, lived Lady Margaret Drummond-Hay and her three children, two girls and a boy; the eldest was Jane, who was slightly younger than I, then came Malcolm and the baby Annalie. My mother and I were old friends of both families, for Mother had often played polo with them and we had enjoyed frequent visits to Ferne for gymkhanas.

During the summer before the Duchess launched her school at Ferne, the Drummond-Hays, at Dennis Farm, became my hosts. And life at the farm soon seemed well-nigh perfect, since not only had Pixie been sent there, for her own safety and my peace of mind, but there were innumerable horses and ponies for us children to care for and ride. Among the best-natured was a pony known as Miss Muffet; she was bred to a horse called Malice and they produced two delightful offspring, Tuffet and Spider. At the farm, Jane and I helped to break them in and generally accustom them to the "playing about" which is good for all young ponies. Dennis Farm also looked after a large number of polo ponies, which we would ride vigorously day after day, usually bareback.

One day, Lady Margaret said: "You two had better make yourselves useful. Why not bring ponies in from the Common?"

It seemed a pleasant and simple enough task to trot the few miles to Semley Common, but when Jane and I

45

arrived we found that the job meant riding our own ponies while leading four others—and we were still riding bareback. It turned out to be an extremely exacting test for a pair of schoolgirls aged ten and eleven; at one stage, Jane and I were not so much "leading" our respective quartets of horses as being entangled and surrounded with all eight. But it was an intriguing pastime, and next evening, when we had sorted ourselves out after a similar mix-up, we devoted ourselves to learning the knack of keeping control. A week later we reckoned ourselves, if not old hands at the job, then at least twice as competent, and unconsciously we were all the time absorbing a first-rate grounding in horsemanship.

And, of course, there was Pixie, who did not go neglected because of my new *richesse* in animals. I rode and schooled her each day, and jumped her, too, in the nearby paddock, where there was a collection of small fences. Jane and I—she mounted on Guinness, her own pony—showed off to each other our ideas on approaches and take-off, and argued strenuously about the technique of jumping.

At breakfast one morning Lady Margaret announced a surprise.

"Ronald is coming to stay for a few days," she said. "Are you pleased?"

I nodded, and reddened slightly, for I was trying to hide the intensity of my pleasure at the news. All day I walked around with a secret elation, without understanding its reason, which was, of course, that Ronald was the symbol of our separated family, and his coming gave me the old sense of unity we had known.

His own school had evacuated even farther west, to

46

Newquay, in Cornwall. When he arrived at Dennis Farm I became more conscious than before of the gap in our ages; he was now a mannish fourteen, and, what was more, had lost all his childish enthusiasm for horses and riding. From the start his stay seemed fated for anti-climax, and he did not hide his disappointment that there was no room available for him at the house. I could easily have wept for him as I watched him receive the cheerful declaration that a "lovely little room" had been furnished out of . . . the stallion's box. Poor Ronald! I helped him carry his case to the stables (where, to be truthful, the horsebox had been made extremely comfortable). But Ronald was no longer "horsy," and to make matters worse there were two doors leading from his bedroom box, one into the stable yard and the other into the stallion's exercising patch; it was therefore rather draughty, and a heavy downpour the previous night had also made it wet.

"I shall have to sleep in my clothes," grumbled Ronald.

"But why?" I asked.

"Because if they lie around here they'll be dripping wet in the morning," he said.

I returned to the comfort of the house, and went to bed with Jane.

Early next morning, I rose, dressed, and went out to see how Ronald had fared. He was standing at the door of the stallion's box, trailing his tie on the ground, and gazing with an expression of deep gloom at a printed enamel plate on the door, bearing the stallion's name: MALICE.

However, Lady Margaret kindly offered to have

Mother and Father and at last we were reunited. But it was only later that I came to realize what a remarkable thing our reunion was, and how much it owed to my Mother's courage and initiative.

Algeria had been a disappointment. My father had enjoyed learning something about Arabs and the desert, but his condition was as painful as ever. He had crossed over into France in the spring of 1940 to try the baths at Aix-les-Bains, but with the German invasion events began to catch up on him.

In London Mother watched the advance of the Panzer divisions with increasing anxiety. I suppose Father, like so many of the French themselves, could not believe that the end had come. At any event, by the end of May it was too late for an arthritic invalid to try to leave the falling house. The Wehrmacht closed in on Aix.

Mother, now desperate, pulled all the strings she could find to get herself a seat on a plane. She succeeded, but by the time she walked into Father's room at Aix-les-Bains, France had fallen to Hitler; on one side the Italian armies were moving in, on the other the Germans were already taking over.

Mother sat up all night, considering all the possible and impossible ways out. Next morning she was out early, and she returned after two hours with train tickets for Lyons and Bordeaux.

"What about permits to travel?" asked Father.

"Oh, the passport control is in frightful chaos. We won't bother about them," she answered.

They headed for the station, which was jammed with refugees. Mother's limitless vigour found a way through to the platform, and half an hour later she and Father

48

Jumping the wall with Pixie at the Richmond Horse Show in 1939 during the competition that gave me my first big win

(*Below*) On Fireworks at Badgeworth in 1941

With Finality at Ostend in 1947 during my first international show
abroad

White City, 1948. Finality had the only clear round for Britain in
her section of the eliminating rounds for the King George V Cup

Harringay, 1949. By winning the first prize, Finality became Leading Show Jumper of the Year

(*Below*) I put in a little practice over our stylish fences at home

(*Above*) Prince Hal at the Western Counties Show, 1951, when he distinguished himself and on this form was selected to go to Madrid with the British team

(*Left*) Her Majesty the Queen, then Princess Elizabeth, presenting me with a rosette at the White City in 1951

were on the train, barely able to shift their feet for passengers and baggage, but with their backs to Aix-les-Bains. At every station more refugees, hundreds exhausted after a night and day of walking, clamoured for places in the already crowded corridors; but on this trip there were no "passengers alighting." Beyond Lyons, the train crawled westward to the coast, a mere four hundred miles away; they reached Bordeaux after two and a half days and were without food for the last twenty-four hours.

Mother bought some bread, cheese, tomatoes and milk before taking Father to the docks, where hundreds of others were also converging. They pushed their way to the quayside to find that small dinghies were already taking refugees to a steamer anchored in the harbour fifty yards away. Father accosted a port policeman.

"What are the chances of getting on that boat?" he asked in his excellent French.

The policeman shrugged as only a Frenchman can, and said nothing.

"Will there be any *more* boats?" Father went on.

The policeman shrugged again, but this time he spoke.

"Perhaps, Monsieur," he said, "but I do not think so."

Father and Mother decided to seek no further useless advice; after much searching they found a dinghy owner prepared to take them, though he could not say whether they would find places on the steamer.

Then the air raid started. Seven or eight German planes came in from the south-east, bombing the town and strafing the harbour and quayside, for the tiny boats were still struggling towards the steamer. Mother and

Father were about to descend the steps to their dinghy when the machine-gun fire raked the quay. Father declared that at last he felt he was "in" the war, but Mother told him to shut up. "Lie down," she called out, "you *must* lie down."

Father argued. "I can't—I'll never get up again if I lie down."

"Do as I say, lie down, I beg you," Mother urged again.

Another plane roared across the harbour. "Why don't *you* lie down?" he called.

"No, I won't," said Mother rudely.

A shade anxious by this time, Father spoke sharply: "Monique, I order you to lie down."

"I will not lie down, so drop the subject," she replied.

Father was now puzzled. "But why, why in heaven's name won't you do as I ask?"

Mother patted her untidy hair.

"This is a brand-new skirt—and I am *not* making it any grubbier."

Father almost collapsed in a roar of laughter. It was a typical reaction from Mother at a moment of high excitement.

But they did reach the steamer, and they did manage to board it. The port policeman had been right—it was the last ship out of Bordeaux; designed to carry two hundred passengers and crew, it sailed out of the harbour carrying fifteen hundred.

Within an hour they were strafed again, and now there were casualties on board and a state of near-panic among many of the more exhausted with their bundles and

50

babies. Mother, the only Red Cross nurse on the ship, went into action with first aid and encouragement. With the captain of the ship she organized an almost continuous feeding rota.

Eventually they reached Falmouth, and the strain began to tell upon Father, who was ill with weariness; the months abroad had been a waste of time and for all practical purposes he would have done better to remain in England. When Mother brought him later to visit us at Dennis Farm, we were unutterably shocked at his appearance.

At the time, as I say, I was perturbed, but hardly able to understand it all. For me, the world was confined to the Duchess of Hamilton's new and remarkable school at Ferne.

We did all our lessons out of doors, apart from the piano lessons I was given by a very amiable Austrian lady, and eurhythmics or "free movement" played a big part in the general curriculum. Along with the Mackintosh children and the Drummond-Hay children I ran barefoot for most of the time—often, indeed, quite naked —hugely enjoying our free exercises and dances on the lawn. The Duchess had great charm; she had also a passion for stray dogs and ponies, and in the park she maintained a home of rest for all and sundry—the horses were poor, wretched old things but doubtless content in the last stages of their retirement.

Riding Pixie and Guinness, Jane and I would often go up to the hills where we held tempestuous races which did no good to our horses. I fear it was by galloping Pixie so hard that I broke her wind. At Ferne, too, we even played polo—a somewhat scratch form of polo, with most of the riders under fourteen years old; in these games I would often ride a pony that greatly resembled Pixie, even to the blind eye.

Most of the time I lived at Dennis Farm with the Drummond-Hays, where Jane and I were kept busy taking the horses back and forth to Semley Common, jumping in the paddock, and learning to break in many of the young ponies which had been bred by Malice, the stallion. This was a fascinating business which taught me a good deal. We were shown the Argentine method of breaking in a young horse, using what is called a *bocado*. This is a small strip of rawhide placed under the horse's tongue and tied under the lower jaw; in this way we saw that we could pull the ponies around without damaging their mouths, and today I still use the same system for "mouthing" a new horse.

Life at Ferne and Dennis Farm was always packed with activity, excitement and mishaps. We were constantly falling off the ponies, or being run away with; at more sober times we helped with the transport, which was mostly by pony and trap; at week-ends we organized impromptu gymkhanas.

One of our friends was Mary Stourton, slightly older and a shade more dignified than us girls who rode bareback wearing nothing but a pair of knickers. Mary was rather better-behaved and considerably more formal— which was perhaps just as well for the child who later became Countess of Gainsborough. She was always properly dressed and preferred to ride side-saddle wearing the proper clothes. She tended to deplore our antics with horses, and when we teased her about her conventional notions she would say: "I *always* ride side-saddle—it's far more graceful." One day when she brought out her side-saddle I helped her make ready one of the ponies; carelessly, we failed to secure the saddle, so that, when Mary mounted, it toppled over the far side, forcing her to dismount somewhat hurriedly. Our hoots of laughter were distinctly cruel.

Jane's mother, Lady Margaret, was at this time teaching riding at Fonthill School, which was not far from Dennis Farm, and after some weeks of carefree activity at Ferne it was decided that Jane and I should become weekly boarders at Fonthill. Here, too, there was a good deal of riding, and Jane and I continued to make ourselves useful by shuttling the horses between Dennis Farm and the school. They were often desperate rides along the country roads, for at times we were each leading as many as eight ponies.

One day we heard that King George VI was coming to inspect the troops who were stationed just below Fonthill; he would be leaving late in the afternoon, and we girls, strongly patriotic, planned to get a glimpse of him when school riding was over. At the end of the riding session, however, it was my job as usual to help in leading the ponies back to the farm. I set off with Lady Margaret and a land girl, each of us with a string of horses.

"If we hurry," said Lady Margaret, "we'll probably be in time to see the King."

Some of the grass verges at the roadside were wide enough for cantering, and we went along rapidly; but, rather more experienced at the job, Lady Margaret and the girl soon outpaced me and disappeared in the distance. I was riding an unusually big horse, leading two ponies on each side. Suddenly, as we cantered, the pair on my right got excited and began pulling and fighting in an alarming fashion. They galloped out into the road and I was forced to follow, but here the two ponies became even more obstreperous, and before long we were all in a chaotic muddle—one horse had even worked his way to the wrong side. I got rather furious and dismounted to sort out the tangle. Then a series of short hoots from a large black car suddenly startled me, and I turned angrily, shouting more to myself than to the driver: "Shut up! Can't you see I'm trying to get these horses out of the road!" Alone with five ponies in the middle of the tarmac, I became tearful, which did no good at all, and kept moaning under my breath: "I shall miss the King. I know I shall miss him."

Eventually I managed to get the ponies under control, led them back to the grass verge, waited for the car to pass and then mounted my big horse. The delay had cost me ten minutes, but we started cantering again and there was no more trouble.

Quarter of an hour later I rounded a bend in the lane to find Lady Margaret, the land girl, and a group of my school friends standing at the roadside chatting. As I drew near they turned and saw me, waved excitedly and chorused:

"Did you see him? Did he wave to you?"

"Did I see who?" I asked, my heart sinking as the truth began to dawn.

"The King, you idiot! The black Daimler that passed you!"

I felt like bursting into tears as I told them my story. It was, of course, the King I had held up in the road— and the King I had totally ignored in my preoccupation with the troublesome ponies. I had not so much as glanced at him, and I could hardly blame the King for failing to acknowledge my back view.

By the end of the year, when the air blitz on London and other towns was in full swing, the Mackintoshes decided to send their four children—Sheena, Vora, Douglas, and Sharloch—to Canada. I stood with the family at the front door of the house at Ferne, saying good-bye. The two small boys were thrilled at the prospect of a voyage across the Atlantic, but Sheena and Vora were in floods of tears. I wept, too—my own family disruption during that year had in fact made a deep impression, and for a long time I was strangely wounded by the sight of departures of any kind.

Most of the time I was feeling intensely homesick for Mother, Father, Ronald, the concerts at Beaufort, the ponies on the Common, and the picnics in Richmond Park. I thought of them all as I lay in bed at Ferne early one summer morning and I could hardly bear it. Outside, except for the occasional crow of a cock, everything was still as the first rays of dawn bathed the quiet downs in early light. The lovely stillness called me. A sudden compulsion came over me and I climbed out of bed, put on some clothes, and crept stealthily downstairs, carrying my shoes to avoid making a noise. It was quite against the rules at Ferne but I carefully unlatched the kitchen door and went out of the house.

It was deliciously fresh outside and the sky was a cloudless blue-green ocean of tranquillity. I walked silently across the yard, collected a halter and ran to the paddock where Pixie was grazing. As I approached she looked up and whinnied a friendly welcome to me. It took a minute or two to catch her and then, after putting a halter round her neck, I climbed aboard.

Out of the paddock and away from the farm, Pixie took me high up to the ridge called Win Green, where the morning sky was brighter and the wind icy. For twenty minutes I galloped Pixie along the broad hill with a great feeling of freedom. Then we stopped, and I looked out over the counties. Far, far away were the Cotswold Hills, and on that December day I did not know that before long I would be riding and living among them.

CHAPTER 4

LATE NIGHT FINAL

UNDER the Devil's Table, nine miles from Cheltenham and nine from Gloucester, we found our new home on the edge of the Cotswolds at the beginning of 1941. Its name was Crickley Lodge, a rambling house and garden owned by Mrs. Butt-Miller, who had won the Derby with her horse Mid-day Sun. Mother had hunted high and low in the district for a place where Father and I could lead a more settled existence, for the sake of health in his case, for the sake of a more steady education in mine; and she was overjoyed, therefore, when she was able to move into Crickley to begin rebuilding the comforts of home and family which had been lost for two years.

I said good-bye to my friends at Fonthill, to Jane and the Drummond-Hays, to the Duchess of Hamilton at Ferne and to the pathetic old horses in her Home of Rest, dispatched Pixie to Crickley Lodge, and started school as a day-girl at Pate's Grammar School in Cheltenham. Although I had enjoyed my months of happy-go-lucky education, I soon found distinct advantages in going to school in fine new buildings, with well-equipped classrooms and laboratories. I bicycled nine miles each morning to school, puffing my way up Crickley Hill and sailing down Leckhampton Hill; at night, loaded with

57

my "prep", the game was reversed and I puffed up Leckhampton and sailed down Crickley. Life was exceedingly busy—and happy.

Crickley lay on the side of an escarpment where the steep fields (in Cotswold language called "banks") dropped nine hundred feet from top to bottom. On these banks we kept the ponies; by now we had acquired quite a "stable", with Pixie, another chestnut mare called Malta (given to us by the Drummond-Hays), Fireworks, who had belonged to my Uncle Gordon, and several of Uncle's polo ponies. We also kept a cow, a Guernsey named Delphine, who was in my charge; before school, I would feed and milk her, and do so again in the evening.

One Saturday morning I went to Father's room for a chat; he was then recovering from a particularly severe attack of arthritis and had announced that for the first time in several weeks he was feeling more cheerful. Mother was there, and so was the doctor, who was giving Father a lengthy examination. Suddenly, Father pushed the doctor away, pointed out of the window to the garden, and shouted:

"Quick, fetch the gun and let me have a go at that pheasant!"

The doctor, with whom we were fortunately on friendly terms, laid a hand on Father's shoulder and smiled.

"Forget it, old boy," he said, "you couldn't possibly fire from this position."

Father sighed, and said: "I suppose you're right, drat you. It was only my sporting instinct showing itself."

Then his eyes brightened as he added:

58

"But why waste the pheasant? Go on, doctor, why don't *you* have a go?"

Perhaps because he understood a little of Father's momentary rush of the spirit of adventure, the doctor smiled again, and said: "This is all highly unprofessional—but dammit I *will* have a shot."

The two men laughed, excited as schoolboys. Mother dashed to a corner cupboard and produced the gun, loaded it, and handed it to the doctor. The pair of them then sped from the house, across the garden, where the doctor stood and took a careful aim. Father and I watched the entertainment from the window, greatly amused at the sight of a stethoscope still draped around the doctor's neck. The gun cracked, and an instant later Mother and the doctor gave a loud cheer—we realized at once that he had made a kill.

Mother retrieved the pheasant while the doctor returned to Father's room, pretending to resume the examination as if nothing had happened. It seemed that the whole incident had done more good for Father than most of the "cures" he had tried, and when the doctor had gone, I stayed to talk.

"I want to ask you something, Daddy," I said. "Can a woman be a farmer—not just a land girl, but a proper farmer?"

"Of course she can," said Father, intrigued. "Why?"

"Because I've made up my mind. That's what I want to be—a woman farmer. With hundreds of horses and cattle."

I explained, haltingly, that the new friends I was making in the nearby farms, the good air of the hills, the sight of the ponies in our field and the farm horses all round—even Delphine the cow—had given me a great longing to own and manage a farm.

Father was impressed, treated my solemn approach with the greatest respect, and said:

"I've an idea—why not ask some of the farmers round about if they would like you to help at week-ends, or in the holidays? You might even earn some pocket money, and you'd certainly get some wonderful experience."

This plan, which had never struck me, seemed perfect, and after obtaining Mother's agreement I saddled Pixie and went for a ride. We visited several farms, and I was surprised to find that more than one farmer was quite taken with the idea that a young and very serious school girl should be offering her services as a labourer.

"Mind you, I'll be expecting a seventy-hour week from you," said one. He gave a deep throaty guffaw, and I was not altogether sure what he had meant.

During the next school holiday I went to work, and this was no mere holiday diversion but real work. At one place there were fifty to sixty cows to milk, morning and night, and only a boy, an old man, and me to do the job. The milking, all by hand, took a long time, then we mucked-out the sheds, and the working day was in full swing. At night, milking again. I received fourpence, it may have been fivepence an hour; but I was rich in experiences. At another farm I passed peaceful hours at the job of harrowing a field, or bank; with a couple of placid old horses, pulling heavy chain harrows, I saw how satisfying was the sight of a field where the molehills were being flattened, and the earth tidied into narrow stripes with a different colour for each wide sweep of the field. Halfway through the day I brought out my bread and a chunk of cheese, a flask of tea and a large apple and lay by the hedge as content as any country philosopher of twenty-five years' standing. Yes, it was a great time for thinking—even at twelve and a quarter.

Things were not easy, financially, at home, for Crickley's charm was a costly affair, and the bills flowed in at an alarming rate. When spring came and the large vegetable garden began to thrive, Mother and I sat down with pencil and paper to work out a scheme for aiding the household expenses.

"It's high time Pixie went into war work," said Mother.

She then disclosed that she had arranged a "deal" in vegetables with several hotels and restaurants at Cheltenham and other places. Starting at once we would break Pixie in to harness, put her into the Raleigh trap and drive her into town loaded with our garden produce. A week or two later, Mother and I rose at dawn one Saturday morning, lifted lettuces and cabbages and set off with our first load. The enterprise became a great success, and later I was allowed to do the journey alone, calling at the hotels, where Pixie would be tied to the nearest lamp-post while I unloaded the lettuce, feeling that intense irritation which comes to children whenever adults smile indulgently at the sight of a child performing a job of work with serious concentration. On these trips, the return journey to Crickley was a gay business, passing the time of day with people on the road, and singing as we bowled through the country lanes—very different from the outward journey, fully loaded, when I often had

61

to climb out of the trap to hold it back on a steep down-hill run, or even help Pixie along with a push on the uphill roads. There was no nonsense from her when she was in harness, and she worked hard.

Despite the market garden earnings, paying our way at Crickley Lodge remained a problem, and soon it was decided that we would turn at least part of the place into a guest house; it could hardly be a major commercial venture since the house was not large enough, and our first paying guests were relatives or family friends. About this time, too, my cousin Sheila—Sheila Curtoys —came to stay with us. Four years younger than I, Sheila was the daughter of one of Mother's three brothers, Hugo, a brave, good-humoured rugger blue whose weight was reduced from sixteen to seven stone as a result of life in a Japanese prison camp. Later in the war, Hugo succeeded while still a prisoner in disorganizing an important electric power installation—a feat which did not improve his treatment by the Japanese prison guards.

Sheila's arrival at Crickley had two important effects; one was that I began to feel protective towards her, which was doubtless good for both of us; the other was that she sometimes took me very happily back to the fantasy life of schoolgirl games, which in my new work-aday world I had tended unconsciously to forget. Behind the house was a small, closely-knit wood where we played, and where we took possession of certain trees. These would become our respective "houses", and we would issue invitations to tea, a game which involved boiling a kettle on a wood fire at the base of the tree, then climbing dangerously to the "house" at the top without spilling things. The pretence would invariably concentrate on the notion of making a "home" and was clearly a feeling of some intensity for both of us. But there was always work to be done, too, and as the months passed I became increasingly devoted to the idea of farming as a career. With Delphine the cow, one of my tasks was to lead her at the crucial time to the nearest bull—which was, unfortunately, four miles away. More than once Delphine, who had a frisky sense of humour, escaped from me and it was not always easy to catch her. Her first two calves were both bulls and it was some time before we were able to congratulate her on giving birth to the heifer we called Christine.

I began learning the tricks of rabbiting, shooting, and ferreting, and adored the excitement of it all. Yet the essential work of farming appealed to me even more strongly, and during the hay-making season I was enraptured by the experience of making wine-cocks of the hay; there had been a good deal of rain during the spring, which meant that hay everywhere had to be cocked and left to dry off in the fields; then, a week or two later, we began carting it. A chain was wrapped around the base of the wine-cocks, and Pixie was set to work pulling them to one end of our Crickley field. Watching from a distance, it was impossible to detect the hidden chain: it seemed that some magical force was moving the beautifully-shaped wine-cocks slowly across the land, or that the mounds of hay themselves were alive.

And, of course, there was riding and jumping—always jumping. First, there was the jumping with cousin Sheila. We would organize contests on the lawn, hurd-

ling deck-chairs and fruit boxes—using only our legs—
and although it was an innocent enough pastime we
invested it, I thought, with at least one original flavour;
we carefully timed each other around the home-made
course in the pretence that our game was a major international competition. Sheila was young enough to be
delighted with it all, and I was by no means old enough
to feel too superior for such pranks.

All the time, I rode and trained and jumped my ponies
—in particular the two which I soon began entering for
gymkhana and country show events: Fireworks and
Malta. I joined the Cotswold Pony Club, enjoyed their
trail rides, hunter trials, and rallies, suffered a thousand
minor falls, and learned a little more each day. One
afternoon, when a half-dozen friends came to tea, I was
being a shade too exhibitionist as I entertained them
with a display of trick riding on Malta, the chestnut
mare. In the middle of a dramatic and perilous movement—brilliantly sensational, I daresay, if it had succeeded—where I was sitting back to front on Malta's
loins, she decided to register an objection, bucked me
violently over her head and I sailed six yards through the
air to land in a soft pile of lettuces which had been carefully laid ready for the market.

News of the most serious fall I foolishly kept from
Mother and Father, to my ultimate cost. Not far from
the house, I was schooling Fireworks over a solid fence
(essential for good schooling with any horse) and we
were both feeling very satisfied with the experience.
Suddenly, however, Fireworks crashed the top of the
fence and fell, landing fairly heavily on top of me. My
ribs ached as I rode her home, and after ensuring that the

64

eona leaping the six-bar gate during the *Daily Mail* Championships at the White City International Horse Show in 1951

(*Above*) Tosc
winning th
North of Eng
land Cham
pionship a
Blackpool i
1952

(*Left*) O
Prince Hal
Miserden
1951

mare was none the worse for the accident, I entered the house. Guilt, or pain, or both, must have been writ large on my face, for Mother looked sharply at me and said with some suspicion:

"*What* have *you* been doing, young lady?"

"Nothing at all, just playing," I lied. "But I've got an awful tummy ache. I think I'll go to bed."

Mother looked surprised, but said nothing, and after I had washed and undressed she brought a glass of hot milk and a biscuit to my room. I told her I felt a little better, kissed her good night, and she left. When she tiptoed quietly into the room three hours later, I pretended to be sleeping, though in fact I was wide awake —with pain. I did not dare reveal that Fireworks had thrown me, for I was convinced that Mother would at once forbid me to jump solid fences, and since I was already planning to enter competitions involving fences just as solid, I kept the discomfort to myself for the three weeks that elapsed before the pain in my ribs finally subsided. Years later, when I was touring abroad and jumping in international events, I still received an occasional twinge of pain in the same spot. A doctor told me I had probably damaged a rib that day at Crickley, and prompt medical attention would almost certainly have set it right in next to no time. So perhaps it is better to face the music—even at the age of thirteen.

Then came Finality—the foal of a milk-cart mare and a thoroughbred stallion—who in the years to come was to bring me more joy, thrills, laughter, and heartbreak than any horse I had known.

Finality was really the outcome of a sensational scene which took place one autumn day in the High Street at

Tunbridge Wells, where a milkman's horse kicked her cart to pieces before a crowd of astonished housewives and shopkeepers. Kitty, the milk horse, was a greedy, excitable, spirited mare who tended to be a thorn in the side of the local tradesman who owned her. On this day, she went berserk, bucked and kicked her way from one side of the busy street to the other, smashed the cart, sent bottles flying, and spread an ocean of milk all around her. Among the spectators of this drama was a farmer with a sense of humour, and when he observed the milkman's fast-growing despair he neatly stepped in with a commercial proposition. Gazing at the destruction, the milkman was in a mood almost to *pay* for Kitty being taken off his hands, and so the astute farmer got her at a bargain price. Kitty was taken home, where she was put to a thoroughbred. Time marched on, and she produced three foals.

Finality was the third—and the last, for Kitty died soon after her birth from the little weakness which was certain, sooner or later, to be her undoing: over-eating, on this occasion a surfeit of lettuce leaves. Her foal, who was therefore brought up on the bottle, eventually found her way into the keeping of our old friend Johnny Traill and he it was who sent her to us at Crickley when the war had run half its course; it was early in 1943.

Now a three-year-old, Finality arrived in the blackout. The Crickley telephone had buzzed at eleven o'clock when Mother was climbing into bed; nothing had gone right that day, Father having been in great pain and in need of much attention. Mother had spent half the previous night at his bedside, had coped with a series of maddening domestic accidents, and was wholly exhausted. She was almost in tears when a voice at the end of the line said:

"Mrs. Smythe . . . Cheltenham Station speaking . . . a horse has arrived for you . . . we can't keep it here all night, so would you come and collect as soon as possible?"

Mother dressed, saddled Fireworks (we had no car at that time), and rode, half asleep, the nine miles to Cheltenham. Midnight had come and gone when she picked up the three-year-old and began the long homeward trek. When they reached Leckhampton Hill, the trouble started. This was the location of a "haunted" house, where there had been at the beginning of the war a gruesome murder—an unsavoury "torso" crime, with limbs chopped off and buried beneath floorboards. Despite the amused contempt of our rationalist friends, we had learned through bitter experience that the horses would never pass this house without a show of nervous excitement. And so it was on this night of all nights. As they came to the haunted house Mother's pony gave a whinny of alarm, swung round, and tossed her head, and caused Mother to lose her hold on the leading rein attached to the new three-year-old. A second later the horse bolted, and Mother gave chase. It took her half an hour to catch up with the frightened newcomer; it was four a.m. when they reached home.

Next day, Mother told us the story of her adventure in the small hours, showed me the new horse, and concluded:

"So you see, she's a proper Late Night Final."

Thereafter we called her Finality, or Final, and started the difficult process of breaking her in. Difficult indeed with Finality, because she was a gawky green frame of a creature who inspired roars of derision from our friends when they learned that I intended making her my show jumper. One of our visitors, Jock Houston-Boswell, the owner of Rondo and other racehorses, laughed heartily at the sight of Finality and called her "The Box". Child that I was, I was hurt and furious, and wanted to box his ears.

I found that Finality was a most uncomfortable ride, for she seemed not so much one horse as two halves joined by a long back. So many things were wrong about her: she needed a great deal of circling and schooling and would always "lead" with the opposite foreleg-to-hind-leg; her weight was all in front, and I had to teach her to carry her head higher; dismounted, she would never stand still when I held her, but would walk incessantly around me; brought up on the bottle, she retained an affectionate but disconcerting habit of pushing me in the stomach, presumably anticipating her milk.

So much that was wrong . . . but so much that was utterly right. She was sensitive and friendly, responsive and humorous, disobedient, yet able and willing to learn. Perhaps it was the occasional flash of almost human eccentricity, as well as her later brilliance, that brought us so close. When, for example, she was turned out in the field near the chicken run, I would often catch her stealing the boiled potatoes or vegetables or kitchen scraps thrown down for the fowls; and if, as usually happened, the scraps were flavoured with a certain well-known poultry spice, Final would attack her illicit meals with even greater relish, and would then gaze a trifle sheepishly over the fence—her mouth enlivened like a clown's with a wide red rim. At all events I loved her dearly, and was convinced from the start that, box-like or not, she would develop into a show jumper of the first class.

Although, during the summer, I worked Finality and devoted as much time as possible to her training it was not with her that I began the round of Red Cross gymkhanas that became my wartime training ground. This was a time for Fireworks, the fast, brilliant pony who came from Uncle Gordon. Fireworks adored the gymkhanas and went with immense gaiety into everything she tackled. At Musical Chairs she was a genius. The game is not so different from its orthodox counterpart at a children's party, except that you are mounted on horseback, cantering around the ring, galloping to the centre when the music stops, dismounting and sitting on a chair, or a bench or log. Our polo pony schooling gave us powerful advantages, since all polo ponies are trained for riding with one hand, and it was thus that I was able to ride Fireworks and other horses. She soon acquired an uncanny sense of instantaneous speed at the moment when the music ceased, but she was almost equally handy in a hundred and one other gymkhana events—potato races, where you dash to a post, lift a potato from the top, gallop away and drop it into a bucket; musical hats, and sacks, and mystery races; relays and Red Cross "rescues", and the rest. Fireworks was so brilliant that she could carry off the prize not only for juvenile contests but for such things as the Open Musical Chairs. The bob-apple race was another favourite, though I always feared that Fireworks would extract the apple from the bucket before me!

The gymkhanas were an amusing, revealing slice of wartime country life among horse lovers. One had to be extremely tactful, for there were delicate balances of prestige, social niceties, snobberies and jealousies and numerous examples of those old, proud, touchy elements in the character of the English lady busy as a bee as she organizes her country fêtes, her garden parties, her summer "season" of charity events. On one occasion, several hundred printed cards were sent out announcing a rally, or it may have been a gymkhana, to be held at the house of Lady So-and-So. All was not well, however. A day or two later the organizer of the affair received an irate telephone call.

"This is Lady So-and-So. I see your card announces that the pony club will be meeting at my place."

"Yes, indeed, Lady So-and-So," said the organizer. "And it really is most kind of you to offer us this hospitality."

"Hospitality, my dear sir," said the enraged woman. "Do you realize that the card does not say *By Kind Permission of Lady So-and-So*? It's really too bad. I simply won't have them."

The organizer spluttered apologies. "Please don't be too hard on us, Lady So-and-So, and in any case it's now too late to change things. As you see from the card, competitors have already been invited, and asked to bring their halters."

"Their halters!" boomed the lady. "Very well, sir, let them bring their halters . . . and hang themselves!"

Before long I was joyfully putting a pound a week into my Post Office savings account; it was always a rule that I pay my own entry fees at the gymkhanas—usually half-a-crown for each entry—and so it was more than ever essential that I should win enough to continue with them. The first prize was invariably one pound. Malta, the chestnut mare, was also a winner of many gymkhana prizes, but Fireworks was unquestionably the star turn.

Within a few months of her arrival, Finality seemed ripe for some jumping experience in public. I was fourteen, had moved from the grammar school and gone as a weekly boarder to St. Michael's School at Cirencester. My chief desire was to race home at week-ends to ride Finality. During dozens of outings, on which we jumped everything we encountered, Final's ability grew rapidly. Mother had warned me to be careful not to hustle her into trying to do too much and so damaging her confidence, and so I would keep her all the time to small obstacles which she could jump freely and in good style. Our harmony developed as I schooled her, cantered her in small circles over small jumps, and gradually saw that she was learning to accept control and respond to those vital forms of encouragement which are known to a rider as "aids". Finality absorbed the notion that jumping was all in the day's work and not an ordeal to get excited about. Eventually I entered her for her first competition.

It was a Red Cross gymkhana run by Mother, at Witcombe near Crickley, where one spectacle was to be a display of trick jumping. We found, however, that there were not enough horses belonging to other people, aside from our own ponies. So the children of the pony club were mounted for the most part on our horses from Crickley; one of my friends rode Finality, another took

Malta, a third rode Pixie, and I was on Fireworks. There was a big crowd of spectators, all intrigued by the array of trick fences. We set the ball rolling—six young riders, all from the Cotswold Pony Club—by jumping a deck-chair in which a dummy reclined. Next came a cleverly constructed hurdle—with an arch of roses by way of decoration. Then a washing-line hung with everything from babies' nappies to frilly underwear and a pair of men's long pants. Then a tea-table, neatly laid for four. Now the excitement was rising. A large bed containing a stuffed dummy of Adolf Hitler faced us. We jumped him successfully and headed for the final obstacle—fire. Jumping in pairs we sailed across a pole hung with blazing straw, and the crowd was highly appreciative. Finally, with one other girl, I galloped for the bed, from which we pulled out Hitler, raced with him back to the blazing pole and dropped him mercilessly into the fire amid cries of triumph. The grand climax came with the entire team forming a V-for-Victory sign. It was a pleasant way to raise money for a good cause.

But Finality quite disgraced herself in this, her first public appearance. She came to the washing-line, jumped it, failed to pick up her hind legs, and tore down the rope, scattering nappies and lingerie all over the ring while the crowd roared with laughter.

Soon afterwards, I decided to take Finality on a round of local shows, combining these with gymkhanas where I was still riding Fireworks. Mother was extremely co-operative, told me she was now confident in my ability to take care of myself *and* the horses, and allowed me to ride off to country shows often twenty, thirty, even forty miles away. I felt very grown-up.

To reach the more distant plates I would start the day before, riding Fireworks, leading Finality, and carrying on my back a rucksack with food, toothbrush, and pyjamas. As a rule there would be friends on the way with whom I could spend the night, but on several trips I had to stay at small farms, and once we camped—the three of us—under trees beside a stream. They were wonderful days, often passed, conversationally, with no one save the horses, and at the shows I could always rely on Fireworks paying our way with her winnings. Indeed, she had to—since whenever I entered Finality for an open jumping competition the fee was no less than a pound, which was something of a strain compared with the half-crown I laid out for Fireworks in her gymkhana events. And in the jumping, Finality was undistinguished for some time, winning little or nothing; but I was far from disappointed, for we were both winning experience at every step.

One of these summer excursions, alone with Fireworks, brought another kind of experience—one which I shall never forget, perhaps because it was the first of its kind, and at fourteen and a half the first of most things is engraved with importance. We had been to a show some thirty miles away and we were both in high spirits after Fireworks had romped home with two victories. The night was strikingly beautiful and I decided to ride home, calculating that I could reach Crickley by midnight, and hoping to creep to bed without disturbing the household. We set off, and by eleven o'clock had made good progress. Then, when I stopped to eat a bar of chocolate, I was suddenly overwhelmed by the bright stillness around me. The moon was full, there was no wind, and the black silhouette of a church spire was sharp against the sky. I felt moved and happy, and thought I could sense the same emotions even in Fireworks. I know that I consulted her, as if she were a relative or friend entitled to express her opinion; and I said, in effect:

"What about it, Fireworks? Shall we get away from this hard, silly road, and try the fields?"

I have long forgotten if Fireworks gave any signs of understanding, but a few moments later I had unlatched a gate in the hedge, climbed aboard and set off on a gallop under the moon and stars.

We went straight home across country, jumping gates, stiles, and stone walls all the way, with Fireworks inspired and sensing something significant even if it was not the adolescent glow that ran through *my* frame. I sang, recited poems, and talked to the pony. Then I pretended we were on a midnight steeplechase, and that in turn reminded me of the framed print we had at home, depicting the first of all the steeplechases some hundred and fifty years earlier; and I imagined *we* were there, too, Fireworks and I, leading the 'chase of 1792. Nearing home, I was brought back to earth by a rude grunting from a sleepless pig. But it mattered no longer, for Fireworks and I had finished our course, won the race, and jumped our way through history, across the fields, over the gates, under the moon.

The following week-end gave me a pleasurable glimpse of things to come. I took Finality to compete in the local jumping at Cirencester, where she jumped an extremely good round and won second prize. I led her to the well-known judge who was distributing rosettes to the victors, and after shaking my hand in congratulation he turned to Finality, gave her a pat, and said:

"Mark my words, you've got a coming show jumper there." The words thrilled me more than any prize of the season.

But Final had weaknesses, one of which was "dishing", and once this nearly led to disaster. One day, Mother came with me to a local show where, before the jumping began, I wanted to give Finality a little limbering up. Standing nearby was a short, pleasant-looking countryman who obviously knew something about horses, for he ambled across the grass and said:

"Can I be of any help, Ma'am? If you and me hold up one of those long poles the young lady here could try a few little jumps."

It was just what we wanted; Mother thanked him, and they each lifted one end of the long white pole that lay near the hedge. I jumped Finality once, then turned for a second approach. In mid-air, right over the pole, Final swerved and "dished" violently—an ungainly scooping movement—kicked the poor man in the mouth and knocked him flat. Mother and I were horrified; she dropped her end of the pole, I hurriedly dismounted, and we rushed to the injured man's side. He stood up, Mother gasped and cried:

"Heavens! She's knocked all your teeth out!"

Quite undaunted, the countryman looked up and gave a wide toothless grin.

"Oh no she ain't, Ma'am," he lisped. "All she done was to smash my blinkin' plate—and it never fitted me, so I ain't worrying."

Home at Crickley, too, life was full of its usual alarms and excursions. I was still an enthusiast for agriculture,

75

joined the young farmers' club, attended lectures, and even rose to the dizzy heights of joining the young men of the club in judging cattle and heavy horses at weekends when I was home from school. Mother remained busy as ever, managing the horses, the garden, the guest house, and Father, whose condition had not improved.

One Sunday we saddled the ponies and went out riding to show an American friend the charms of the Cotswold countryside. We had gone more than five miles from home when Mother stopped, swayed on her horse, and almost fell off. We helped her to dismount and within five minutes she was on the point of collapse; with great difficulty we carried her back to Crickley. put her to bed, and called the doctor. Before he arrived I took her temperature, for she was sweating and shivering in turn, but decided that the thermometer was broken when I failed to find the mercury. I laid it aside, then snatched it up again as a horrifying thought struck me. This time I looked more closely and saw that it registered a fraction over 105 degrees. Mother had got pneumonia.

For the next fortnight I stayed at home acquiring what now seems like a year's experience of domestic work. Although we had some help, it was a harassing time, involving the day and night nursing of both parents, household chores and cooking for the guests (who rallied to my aid magnificently), caring for the ponies, milking Delphine the cow, tending the vegetables, loading and driving them into town, catching up on school work, and snatching odd moments for schooling and jumping the horses. I got little sleep, and often wonder if those somewhat tough working weeks had some effect on my capacity, years later, for keeping consistently active for eighteen hours a day.

The weeks following Mother's recovery brought us into close contact with the American Forces. We had already entertained a few American officers and other ranks, and now, during the Christmas holidays, a large party were invited to see how the English turned out a traditional Christmas dinner. The soup and turkey were a huge success, the wine and merriment were flowing well, and all went smoothly until Mother entered with an outsize Christmas pudding.

"Somebody pour the brandy over it!" she called above the laughter and hubbub.

Without delay, somebody did. Unhappily, the pouring was too liberal (not an uncommon fault with our American friends), and when the brandy was lit the entire dish went up in flames. The heat spread across the silver tray, burning Mother's hand. As she let out a yelp of pain, the pudding slithered across the flaming dish, toppled gently over the edge and crashed to the polished dining-room floor. A roar of applause greeted this catastrophe, and after making certain that Mother's hand was safely bandaged the entire company solemnly went on its knees to scrape up as many portions of the pudding as were still edible. But the whole afternoon was destined for breakages. One of our guests came in with the coffee tray, slipped on a rug, and landed on the floor surrounded by the shattered pieces of our finest coffee service. Then Mother began demonstrating mashie shots round the hall, using a real golf ball. By now the party was going strong.

"I'll bet you don't hit the ball into that sofa," said a sergeant, pointing to the far end of the hall.

"Done!" said Mother. She took aim and let fly with her club. The ball just touched the top of the sofa before bouncing a foot higher to smash the last picture in our series of old prints depicting the midnight steeplechase. I was sent to fetch a brush and dustpan, we swept up the broken glass and crowded around to examine the print. Poetic justice. Its title was *The Finish*.

We were all profoundly touched when a batch of officers, moving away from the hospital where they had been confined for some months, informed Mother that they would like to make us a gift of their mascot . . . "a little pet lamb". Next day, a three-ton army truck drove up the Crickley drive and spilled out a quartet of Americans who began unloading a wooden crate large enough to hold a small pony. We were astounded when we saw "the little pet lamb". He was in fact an enormous woolly ram, aptly called Hercules, who had been fed for months on the best-quality U.S. Army condensed milk; but we tethered him on the lawn in company with Polly and Artful, our two Toggenburg goats, and the three of them succeeded in keeping down the grass and weeds with such efficiency that the lawnmower was rarely needed.

Early one morning I went out as usual to milk Delphine the cow and was disturbed to find that she was almost dry. At night the same thing happened, and when yet again she gave no milk the following morning, Mother decided to call in a vet. That afternoon, however, I came upon Hercules the ram making determined efforts to emulate Finality by jumping the garden wall

78

into the field where we kept Delphine. It gave me an idea, and next day I rose half-an-hour earlier, went quietly out of the house, carrying the milking pail, and walked stealthily towards Delphine.

From across the wall I watched the answer to Delphine's lactic depression. Like a young calf, Hercules was standing at her side helping himself noisily to her milk for all he was worth. Once again there was little or no milk for us, but from that day forward we made certain that Hercules was kept within bounds.

Among our visitors, too, were some of the young heroes of the R.A.F. who had been badly shattered in the Battle of Britain and the assaults on German cities. Many had artificial legs. These appliances fascinated rather than appalled me, and, extrovert schoolgirl that I was, I shook the R.A.F. boys out of their tea-time shyness by kicking them under the table to discover which was the "tin" leg. Then I would insist on being shown how the various joints worked, and before long the young flyers had lost most of their inhibitions. Nowadays I shudder at the thought of my displays of insensitivity and try to re-assure myself that without knowing it I was helping the process of readjustment for those heroes of Britain.

What of Ronald, who was now nineteen?

He was up at Oxford, having won a major history scholarship before his seventeenth birthday, gone to The Queen's College, and moved rapidly into a world of far too many activities. Occasionally we had spent a sunny week-end with him, boating on the river; once, after Mother's pneumonia, she and I had spent a delightful week meeting his friends and seeing the variety of his doings. He had joined the R.N.V.R. and was preparing for service in the Navy when serious eye trouble post-poned his call-up. Treatment was unsuccessful so he was discharged and after trying his hand at several interim jobs he decided to return to the University, feeling rather out of things but determined to get a good degree. He came home for some of the vacations, and as I was sitting for the School Certificate was able to give me some tips. Mother had wisely decided that I would concentrate better on my work if I became a weekly boarder at St. Michael's School, Cirencester, where I received a very thorough general grounding and a valuable religious education which has been a great stand-by. However, I lived for the week-ends, and many a lesson was passed in the haze of daydreams about jumping paddocks and over Puissance courses. Consequently no one was more astonished than I was to learn that I had matriculated with credits in seven subjects, and so, at the end of 1944, a month after my sixteenth birthday, I left St. Michael's and came home to Crickley to help Mother and to consider the future.

That December my father's arthritic condition was complicated by an attack of pleurisy. Under Mother's devoted care he made an amazing recovery for our last Christmas together, but the effort was too great for him, and on 19 January, 1945, he died.

I went out to the field at Crickley, wandered aimlessly about stroking Pixie and the other ponies, then saddled Finality and galloped away, the tears burning on my cheeks as they dried in the January wind.

CHAPTER 5

INTO THE INTERNATIONAL RING

IT WAS therefore a choice between the comforts of family life at Crickley and the cost of keeping horses in the belief that I would make a show-jumper. What I owe to my mother can be seen from the fact that she did not hesitate to give up Crickley and to move first to her mother's in Bath and then to various temporary quarters ending with a single room in the Blathwayt Arms on Lansdowne, to begin a Riding School by means of which she could support herself and maintain the horses for me. She even did without the help I might have given her for, when some kind relations offered to finance my further schooling, she gladly sent me off to Talbot Heath, Bournemouth, to study for the Higher Certificate. Much though I would have preferred to stay and help her, I could see the value of continuing my education, and as I was more than ever determined to learn about farming I was soon absorbed in science and biology.

At Talbot Heath I was lucky to have the use of a good library where, together with Watson on "Agriculture" (lent by a boy-friend) I compiled over a period of some eighteen months a large notebook of classified information on farming, which I still have.

Though I cannot say that I enjoyed boarding-school life, it gave me an opportunity to improve my piano-playing, to join the school orchestra with a recorder, to play cricket for the first time, to bathe, and to learn new gymnastics, and finally to get some experience of responsibility as head of my school "Hall". There was the New Forest and Branksome Chine (later marred by Heath) for delightful excursions, and I took an occasional, though illegal, trip to the Isle of Wight for a breath of fresh air.

On the windswept heights of Lansdowne above the tranquil dignity of the lovely city of Bath, Mother's riding school gradually took root and blossomed. She was never very comfortable. At one temporary lodging the rain dripped down the walls incessantly, cooking was done on a primus, water had to be fetched from a pump, and the horses had to be content with a cowshed. It was so cold that we would resort to all sorts of devices to keep ourselves and our clothes warm and dry. At the Blathwayt, where we rose to the height of an electric hotplate, the result on one occasion was a pair of well-grilled underwear! There were many discouragements, the most familiar being well-intentioned people who let you down, but the first big shock came from Finality.

I was at Bournemouth, Mother had gone up to London, but Ronald was in Bath visiting his grandmother, when he received a telephone call from Lansdowne saying that one of the horses had broken out and damaged itself. When he arrived he found that the greedy Finality had used her skill to jump into a cornfield. Having gorged herself and made a mess of the farmer's corn, she had tried to get back: but who can rise to the occasion after a heavy meal? In attempting to return she had torn herself badly on wire and now shivered with terrible gashes on all four legs, bleeding profusely. Ronald called the vet and under his instruction bathed the wounds for the rest of the day. On her return Mother took over, but the vet's comment was, "If she does recover she will probably be useful only as a brood mare. I cannot imagine that she will ever be able to jump again."

Happily he underestimated Final's powers for, with the coming of summer her recovery was complete and she was ready to be ridden and jumped again. But for nearly four months my dreams had been agonized pictures in which endless miles of torturing wire had torn at my own limbs as well as Final's.

Pixie was at Lansdowne, of course, but in honourable retirement as the most popular children's pony. She was now very sober and matronly. Our great hope had been that she would consummate her career in marriage, but we brought her to stallions that were aristocrats, to stallions that were strong and silent, to stallions sleek and handsome and all that an equine female could or should desire. But she did not love them. At length to our joy, however, she fell in love unmistakably and absurdly with a small carefree boy of the Welsh hills.

On the day of victory in Europe, just before we left Crickley, Pixie had her foal—a skewbald filly, dubbed Victoria, of course. The victory of the allies had been capped by her own personal achievement.

During the summer holidays Mother and I worked long and hard, the room at the Blathwayt our headquarters. Shopping, cooking, cleaning, washing-up, and generally looking after each other occupied every hour that was not devoted to the horses. But Mother was a brilliant teacher, and soon the riding school began to show small signs of prosperity. At every possible moment I schooled and exercised Finality, and as the weeks passed our partnership of sympathy grew stronger than ever before. Still praying that her escapade had caused no lasting harm, I took her to the Box Show, near Bath, and entered for the Open Jumping competition. She won it, brilliantly and calmly; there was no doubt that Finality was well again. We also entered for several events at the Shepton Mallet show, failed to pull off the jumping, but won the Musical Chairs. The next contest was at Melksham; again Finality won the Open Jumping, and on this day I was equally delighted with her performance in the High Jump. The event was won by the celebrated Tankard, mounted for the first time at a show by Brian Butler, for whose prowess I had an undisguised envy and admiration; never at that time could I have believed that before long Finality and Tankard, with Brian and me aboard them, would be jumping together as members of a British team. Tankard cleared roughly 6 feet at our Melksham show, and later Brian went on triumphantly to win the *Daily Mail* Cup. But I was more than satisfied with Finality's 5 feet 7 inches in the High Jump that day, and I returned to school in Bournemouth for the winter, full of hope for the spring of the following year.

The winter term was uneventful, and at the end I was ready to put schoolgirl life behind me once and for all, though that day was still months ahead. I say uneventful, yet once again the news from Mother had been depressing, for while I was away Finality fell into the pit of misfortune for the second time within twelve months— now, wrote Mother, she had gone down with strangles—

the diphtheria of the horse—and the illness kept Finality out of action until the early summer. Nevertheless, soon after her recovery she was jumping, and winning, once more, and Mother then suggested entering her for a major show. It was nothing less than the Victory Jumping Competitions of the first post-war White City display, a national show for which I felt that both Final and I were now fit.

A few weeks before the great event, a third tragedy reduced me to tears and fury. At some small local show, an obstreperous horse got out of control, galloped head-long into Finality, inflicted a violent kick and gashed one of her hind legs so seriously that all hope for our White City début was ended. By this time the jumping bug, which had long ago entered Final's blood, was firmly embedded in mine, and the frustration of the new calamity was almost more than I could bear.

I went to the White City, gloomily, as a spectator. Fidgeting in the seat, my heart ached to be out in the ring, riding, jumping, and striving with Finality to win a place among the victors. I had almost made up my mind, in impotent desperation, to skip the rest of the proceedings and go out to a cinema when suddenly I realized that I was watching a man, fascinated. This was a horseman, I thought, as I saw the unfolding of a technique which bore the stamp of a master. The event was the Victory Challenge Cup, the horse was called Kilgeddin, and the rider was Harry Llewellyn. It was my first sight of Colonel Llewellyn in action, and it was enough to dispel all the feelings of adolescent hopelessness which had enveloped me that day.

Final's leg healed soon afterwards, and before returning to Bournemouth for my last term at school I jumped her at a number of small shows. By the end of the summer she had won me, in her brief career, a little more than £200. I was also now a member of the British Show Jumping Association.

After celebrating my eighteenth birthday I said good-bye to school friends and came back to Mother, Finality, the Blathwayt, the cooking, and the weighty work with the horses. Mother had made a remarkable job of re-establishing our domestic stability under these trying conditions, and was already talking hopefully about the prospect of our return to Crickley Lodge, where she would rebuild the familiar pattern of the guest house. During my last months at school she had helped to establish the Bath Riding Club, which was later to become one of the most flourishing in the country, and had even managed to buy new ponies for the use of the child riders who came for her expert instruction. These were tough little Welsh ponies bought from gipsies at the Glastonbury Fair, and we had broken them in during the summer. They were kept tethered, by a rope around the neck, on the wide grass verges of the road near the Blathwayt—for we had no other land to house them—and twice a day their grazing patch would be shifted. One of the ponies was an aptly-named youngster called Mainspring, who jumped his way into the oddest predicament I have ever seen, on the day I returned from school. Mainspring's jumping had about it the careless-ness of a flea; he would jump even while tethered at the roadside. To do him justice, however, it was the strident howl of an electric motor horn which pricked him on this occasion. I watched astonished from the window as

86

Mainspring leaped into the air, snapped his tether as if it were cotton thread, sprang into the road, and landed with a mighty crash across the bonnet of a passing car. Luckily the driver was unhurt, and even Mainspring escaped with a cut on his stomach—but the bonnet of the car was caved in like a battered dustbin; the owner, to say the least, was noticeably put out.

Christmas brought an exciting invitation from Lady Jean Mackintosh and her family, who had been at school with me at Ferne. Would I join them, and a party of young people, for a New Year skiing holiday at Zermatt? Not counting an excursion across the Channel at the age of three, it was my first opportunity to go abroad, and Mother agreed that it was too good to miss. We reached Zermatt on New Year's Eve and for the next ten days I revelled in a racy student-life of sport and gaiety which was altogether new to me. Switzerland had not yet got into its post-war stride with the tourist trade, nor yet provided the luxury living to which winter sports addicts were soon to become accustomed. But we had no cares for the comparative austerity of the time, spent our days skiing and climbing, I, for one, black and blue from my bruises in my determination to master another sport. Hearing that all the best skiers fell forward I succeeded in dislocating my thumb in my efforts to keep my weight forward. There was at Zermatt a delightful party of students from Edinburgh. The favourite sport of one young man who frequently escorted me at skiing and dancing was a game which often got us in hot water with the guards of the funicular train. Angus, the student, would collect our skis from the rear of the train, and on the downward journey we would both leap from the crowded box-like carriage when it drew level with our hotel—in order to save the trouble of trudging back from the station. Out for a stroll one evening, rounding a corner near the hotel, we collided with the funicular guard who had shaken his fist at us that morning; he recognized Angus and me at once, and there followed a twenty-minute chase through snowbound Zermatt. Angus and I, hopelessly irresponsible and twenty-five years younger than the irate guard, led the poor man a frustrating dance, and finally escaped. It was altogether a night of good spirits and bad citizenship. Each day, nevertheless, contained one brief period of thought which took me away from the radiance of our youthful party, for I could not stem the rush of sadness that came with the sight of my Father's noble Matterhorn, proudly adorned with a plume of snow blowing from the summit.

When I returned to England in mid-January, conditions around Bath and the Blathwayt were almost Swiss-like. Deep snow covered the land and the English winter was tempestuously exceeding its recognized practices. Events had moved fast since my Alpine interlude, and Mother had almost completed the arrangements for our return to the Cotswolds. When the snow abated she left for Crickley to make the house ready and prepare for guests once more. I was to follow four days later.

But then the snows returned, in full fury. In those four days we became blockaded by snow, and my journey was out of the question, since the horses, in the racehorse stables near the Blathwayt, could not now be moved by any normal methods of transport. Living alone in my room at the inn, I was kept busy from morning until dusk—for six weeks, through a biting February and on into a windy March. Snow or not, the horses still had to be exercised and fed, so there was nothing for it but to take them into the white fields where I worked them every day. Even their feed and water had to be carried in buckets, for the snow was too deep to get at the grass. For several days the storm raged incessantly, and in the glistening light of each snowy morning I would dig the drifts away from the stable doors, enough to extract the horses and lead them out for exercise.

In some places, by the end of the first week, the snow drifts were fifteen feet deep, and Lansdowne was totally marooned. A villager arrived at the Blathwayt one morning with the news that Lansdowne families were almost out of provisions. We held a solemn strategic conference and decided that sledge-and-pony would be the answer to the siege. I had already harnessed a pony to a sledge loaded with hay for the horses in the nearby fields, and now the rescue service took on a more serious task— skimming through the lanes to the hill above Bath, collecting bread and groceries, and returning with a feeling of victorious *élan* on the sleigh-drive which I called the Relief of Lansdowne.

By the middle of March I was able to contemplate the trip to Crickley, arranged for the horses to be moved by cattle lorry, said good-bye to our friends at the Blathwayt Arms, and went home to join Mother. This English winter had not been dull.

Nor was it dull at Crickley, where the snow had been equally heavy and where the shortage of water now became more desperate than usual. Crickley's water supply was a well that habitually dried up in summer, froze up in winter, and behaved temperamentally at most other times. When I reached home Mother's greeting was that of a parched shipwrecked mariner.

"Water," she said. "For goodness' sake get me some water."

I knew exactly what she meant, went out to harness Pixie to the trap, struggled to heave our large portable tank safely inside it—and drove a mile through the slush to get water from a spring at the far end of the road.

Among the major irritations of life at this time was the fact that I looked about two years younger than the eighteen I boasted, and as every girl knows, nothing is more galling than to be smiled upon as a child at those very moments when one feels oneself to be more than usually mature, emotionally if not in other ways. And so the history of my driving lessons, and in particular of my driving tests, was with me an exceedingly sore point. I had in fact been driving cars, motor-cycles, vans, trucks, tractors and trailers, with and without horse boxes, since the tender age of fifteen. Most of my driving had been in other people's vehicles, since most of the time we had not owned a car: but of one thing I was certain—by the time I had reached eighteen I was, I considered, as fitted for the official honour of a driving licence as any motoring man or woman in the country. I squirmed, therefore, when the inspector of my *first* driving test, a gloomy, spectacled, dwarf official who seemed to resent his own small stature, growled at me:

"And how old are you, might I inquire?"

"I'm eighteen," I said, bristling indignantly. The little man took an obvious and immediate dislike to me, surpassed only by mine for him.

"And where is the vehicle?" he went on, sourly.

"Just here," I answered, my hopes sinking as I pointed out the small, scarred, aged van which had been our second-hand maid-of-all-work for some months.

The inspector alternately sighed and snorted. "Must I really carry out a test in that filthy thing?"

I said nothing, but climbed into the driving seat and invited him to join me. Like many such vans, this one had only a single fixed seat for the driver, the rest of the front accommodation being a loose bucket seat which was useful though far from comfortable. However, he settled himself on it without comment and away we went.

The next fifteen minutes provided enough catastrophe to create what I am certain is the worst human relationship that ever existed between an inspecting official and a novice driver. We bowled along without incident for perhaps ninety seconds. Then the inevitable occurred; a trifling dent in the road surface rattled the van to its unsure foundations and, as always happened, the doors flew open. The inspector glowered. I laughed somewhat lamely. Three hundred yards and a dozen scowls later, we jerked to a stop on the crest of a hill. It seemed that there was water in the petrol; the inspector glowered again. I managed to start, and at the next bend we came to a low bridge.

"Have you any idea," he sneered, "what to look for when you approach a low bridge?"

I answered brightly. "Oh, yes, look carefully for high

vehicles driving in the centre of the road and coming from the opposite direction."

Altogether too brightly, for he looked up sharply and said:

"You're the first person I've known to answer correctly—how do you know all that?"

"From experience," I began—and suddenly clapped a hand over my mouth as I realized his dawning suspicions that I had illegally driven high lorries at an age when it was an offence to do so. He issued a severe warning, and glowered again.

Three minutes later he called out:

"Now stop!"

Why should I be blamed (I complained later to Mother) for brakes that were too good? A trifle startled by his sudden order, I pulled up sharply, and an instant later I gave a loud, irreverent roar of laughter as the loose bucket seat hurtled backwards, somersaulting the outraged official into the rear of the van. The last straw was neatly provided when the back door swung open. The *débacle* was complete.

"If you think you're getting a 'Pass' from me, you're sadly mistaken. Next time see that you provide a vehicle fit to take the road," said the inspector, dusting himself. Poor man—in retrospect I became almost well-disposed towards him. All this had taken place at Bristol, for I had applied for the test before leaving Bath. The next attempt, however, was thoroughly successful. I borrowed a friend's brand-new limousine for the occasion.

By April, 1947, the guest house at Crickley was thriving again. I persevered with Finality's training, until a temporary setback put Mother, me, and half the household in bed. A small boy among the guests developed chicken-pox.

Mother and I succumbed badly and threatened to infect the entire neighbourhood by intermittently leaving our beds to attend to the work of house and horses. One result of the household epidemic was that Finality had to go unworked for more than a fortnight, and when I was fully recovered and ready to jump her again she was inevitably frisky, full of excitement and athletic spirits. I took her out one afternoon, over to the common where I jumped her across the logs and fallen tree-trunks. Suddenly Final bucked hard and threw me high into the air. I came down with a twist, landed heavily on one hip and passed out. I recovered consciousness, caught Final and rode dizzily home. The effect of this fall was lumbago— an ailment which until then had rather bored me when its victims talked of their pains in the back. At eighteen I learned the truth about lumbago, and never again dismissed it lightly.

By the end of April I was fit enough to consider a programme for Finality's summer jumping, though I did not imagine that her rise to fame would be quite so sudden and spectacular, nor that her future and mine would be decided within a few weeks. In May, at Cheltenham, we entered for the important Bath and West Show, where Mother and I were delighted and astonished to find vast crowds of enthusiastic spectators; indeed, I realized for the first time that show jumping in England was fast turning into a spectator sport of the first rank—by four o'clock that day more than twenty thousand visitors had arrived, and by the end of the second day the show had clocked in a record total of no less than fifty thousand, a remarkable figure for an agricultural district.

Finality jumped superbly throughout the show and was brought to the notice of those whose names and achievements matter in the world of show jumping. Her effort was described as a "refreshing performance, with a style and pace worthy of an international event"; we went home to Crickley, highly satisfied, and now eager for the first international show of my life—the White City in July.

Never was a mare more hunted by the demons of misfortune, nor fuller of heart and courage in fighting them. A week or so before the White City International, Finality went lame. This time she had contracted a heel bug disease, and for the second year in succession it seemed that our chances would collapse. But this time we were luckier; a skilful vet produced a rapid healing of the condition, and by 8 July—the day before the show—Finality was pronounced fit for jumping.

Jump she did, and with such success that twenty-four hours after returning home I was gazing incredulously at an invitation to join the British show jumping team for the international events in Belgium at the end of the month.

I could hardly believe it to be true and I wandered around in a dream all day. I imagined thrilling competitions with Finality jumping off against Marquis III, the winner of that year's George V Cup. In actual fact, M. d'Oriola would have had no doubts whatever about the superiority of Marquis III over Finality in any speed competition. However, my faith in Finality was supreme, and although I had grave misgivings about my own ability to compete against the foreigners I felt sure that she would carry me through. Finality had made her mark as a possible international jumper and also incidentally made her mark on Mother's best hunting boots, which I had borrowed, by treading on my toe and leaving the imprint of a large jumping stud.

At this time Britain had barely cut her milk, much less her wisdom, teeth in the fast-growing schools of competitive show jumping among the nations. Early in 1947 a team was sent abroad for the first time to compete in international events; first at Nice, then at Rome, we began learning how little we really knew. But now there came right to the forefront a determined and energetic Welsh colonel with a genius for organization and inexhaustible funds of enthusiasm . . . Harry Llewellyn, the leader in every sense of the word. He had recently acquired a new horse. He called it Foxhunter.

We set off for Belgium—Ostend and Le Zoute were the battlegrounds—at the end of July. The British team, headed by Llewellyn (with Kilgeddin and Foxhunter), consisted of Ruby Holland-Martin (with High Jinks and Tallycoed), Toby Robeson (with Rufus II), Brian Butler (with Tankard) . . . and me (with Finality).

The horses were shipped separately and housed at Ostend in the racecourse stables, which were strikingly smart and well-equipped—a distinction notably lacking in our hotel. During the first two days of our visit we became increasingly alarmed at the quantities of salami and unattractive cold meats which the Belgian proprietor seemed to regard as the sole requirement of the British if not the human stomach. The team decided to brave the situation with a blend of typical British stoicism and typical British humour. We posted several kilos of salami in the nearest letter box.

In the competitions, the team put up a creditable display, and I was relieved that Finality went well; indeed she won her first international cup, which was not unsatisfactory in view of our inexperience at international shows; but that victory meant rather less to her than the experience of a paddle in the sea; it was her first direct contact with salt water, and she paddled, skipped, and jumped the breakers with such an air of girlish excitement that at any moment I expected to hear her deliver a loud squeal and deposit me in the drink.

At Le Zoute we were all made extremely comfortable in a first-class hotel; there was a dance at night, and conversation with French partners renewed my determination to improve my School Certificate standard of languages; quite inexplicably, I remember making a mental note during a tango that whenever I might have children, they too would be encouraged, even forced to become multi-lingual.

The jumping in next day's international events—the *Concours Hippique Internationale de Zoute*—was marked in my memory for two reasons. The first was Tankard's understandable resistance to what was for us an extraordinary fence: a bank constructed of sandbags with a post and rails at each side and a deep ditch into the bargain. The idea was that you jumped over ditch, post and rails, on to the sandbank, then down from the bank, over post and rails again, across the ditch and out to the ground the other side. My friend Brian Butler seemed to be going well on Tankard, and jumped beautifully until he came to the sandbag fence, where Tankard

In the stable yard at home, at Miserden. I am mounted on Tosca and leading Prince Hal and Candy

Tosca winni
the Selby Cu
at the Whi
City in 195

(*Below*) Leo
at the Whi
City, 1951

threw Brian surely and hard, into the bottom of the ditch.

Alarmed, we made a dash for the fence, for Brian did not get up, and it seemed certain he was badly hurt.

When we reached the open ditch, we looked anxiously, ready to spring for first aid and an ambulance. We need not have worried. Butler was reclining at the bottom of the ditch as if he were enjoying a lazy Sunday morning in bed; he opened his eyes to say, with a ponderous sleepy impudence:

"Go away, all of you . . . don't disturb me . . . I'm so comfortable in here."

The second incident concerned the final competition, which we were all desperately keen to win. Finality had already done well in the puissance event, and while waiting for our next and last testing battle, I was chatting in the members' tent, lounging in comfort on a pile of stretchers as I sipped a glass of champagne. A vague feeling of annoyance swept over me as someone passed by and remarked casually:

"Hope you're not on that stretcher to-night."

I looked around, but the voice had gone. Quickly I finished my champagne as the bell rang, borrowed a mirror from a pretty French waitress, gave myself a dab of lipstick and hurried away to collect Finality for the big event.

It was late when the jumping began, and by the time a number of good fast rounds had been jumped, I noticed that the sun was a bright red glow, slipping down, inch by inch, into the distant trees. I was the last of our team in this event, and I knew that time was what counted . . . the fastest clear round, and though some had been fast indeed, I felt a sudden determination that Finality's would be the fastest, clearest, and finest of them all.

She jumped like a stag, smooth and fast in every step she took, cutting the corners superbly and doing what must certainly have been the fastest time of all.

Until the last fence.

I cannot swear to what happened; probably the sun, a rich fiery shade by then, got into her eyes; spectators said that so far as they could judge the horse did not seem even to see the last fence. Finality turned a double somersault over it, and we both fell heavily. After that, purple-black swooning emptiness.

From the nearby bar tent, they brought the stretcher that lay on top of the pile, placed me gently upon it and carried me away.

Out cold on the stretcher, cold as cooled champagne, but with no champagne glass in my hand.

CHAPTER 6

A POUND IN MY POCKET

ON MY nineteenth birthday—following our début with the British team in 1947—I coined what I felt to be a profound philosophical truth. Life, I decided, is like jumping. Peaks of exhilaration after a satisfying take-off and a good clearance are offset by sudden, sinking tragedies which range in intensity from the minor fall without bruises to the full, awful crash with multiple injuries. Trite or not, the soundness of this youthful epigram was to be proved within the next twelve months, for by the end of a fine summer, when all had seemed right with the world, I was to lose in quick succession a favourite boy friend, our home at Crickley—and, deepest wound of all, Finality.

Pale but unruffled after my undignified exit from the ring in Belgium, I returned to England to jump Finality with considerable success in a busy round of small shows. Then, in the winter, we acquired our first point-to-point horse, a handsome bay thoroughbred called Dandy Dick. We hunted several times, and in the spring of 1948 he raced and gave me my first point-to-point experience—but all these were months of interlude, leading to the shows where, once more, Finality revealed her quality. Like all show jumpers of the first rank, she loved her jumping and was always glad to begin a new season.

Her successes of the early summer reached a fine climax
—and brought a cruel blow—on 26 June at Salisbury.
Final had jumped brilliantly throughout every day of
this Royal Counties Show, and now, on the last day, we
were competing for the Walwyn Challenge Cup, a
national championship event of some significance.

Before the contest began, I stood talking with Mother
and a friend while Finality, a yard or two away, preened
herself in the sun. Then, as the event was announced
over the loudspeaker, Final moved peremptorily into
our group and gave me a firm push in the stomach—that
odd but engaging habit which she had retained from the
days when she was fed by the bottle. On this of all days
it seemed to me like a gesture of impatience . . . to win.

An hour later she pushed me once more in the stomach
and the assault seemed altogether gentler and more
affectionate. But by that time the Walwyn Challenge
Cup was hers.

Then the blow fell. Since the day Finality had first
come to us, in the dark of night and the darkness of the
war, we had always been a shade apprehensive about her
future; for one thing, she was not wholly our property,
having been placed in our keeping by our old friend
Johnny Traill, and although her life and abilities had
grown up with Mother and me, the question of her
ultimate disposal did not rest with us. And so, despite
our financial interest in Final—which was as nothing
compared with our love for her, and her attachment to us
—she was sold to a new owner on that June night when
we had jumped our fences to victory for the Walwyn
Cup.

At first, when Mother announced that Final must go,

I refused to believe it; then, when the force of the news penetrated my confusion, I wept until it seemed that no more tears were inside me; and finally, when our partnership was firmly ended by her departure from Crickley, I felt that my jumping career was over.

Finality went to Castleford, Yorkshire, into the stables of Mr. Tommy Makin, himself one of the most brilliant of Britain's show jumpers in his youth. Depressed and lonely, I carried on with an effort to make ends meet by jumping other horses—other people's horses, novice horses, borrowed horses, young horses of our own that Mother had brought from Ireland during a visit the year before, horses good, bad, and certainly indifferent, though none so indifferent as my own feelings towards them. I persisted, nevertheless, and won sufficient to pay our expenses.

There was a single bright ray attending Finality's sale; we had been able to enforce the condition that I should jump her in the White City events during August of that year, having entered for the show before she was sold. So Final came back to me, for just a week, and although I can truthfully say that I have never felt maudlin about animals—indeed, I loathe the maudlin attitude—I was again moved to tears by the clearly pathetic character of her pleasure at returning. She came to Crickley, took possession of her old stable, whinneyed every time that Mother or I took a step within earshot, and was soon full of good spirits. Then we drove her to London, ready for the battles that we both knew so well.

During the time of the White City Show, we kept Finality at Richmond, where, incidentally, she received the severest shock of her life at her first sight of a deer.

an experience which made her jump with surprise rather than style. And at Richmond, too, I rode and schooled her—my first jaunt in that Royal Park since the pre-war days of my schoolgirl games and gallops. Here, Final was not so sentimental over our reunion as to be unwilling to try bucking me off. As we cantered along, several deer came in sight a hundred yards or so away, whereupon Finality bucked backwards and sent me straight over her head. I managed to hold on to the reins so that at least she could not escape, but it was all a monstrous humiliation and I was thankful that no one saw the spectacle.

Then, next day, to the White City for the International Horse Show of 1948, a few months before my twentieth birthday.

Nothing could have shown more conclusively that Final was *my* horse and I *her* rider. She had never jumped well for anyone else, and continued to perform indifferently as soon as we again parted. But at least for that White City Show we were our old selves, confident whatever the outcome, and with a great joy in our harmony. She jumped a brilliant clear round in the preliminaries for the King George V Cup, and thus went into the finals, in which she was joined by Ladybird, who was ridden by Lulu Rochford; this was an unfortunate day for Finality, for she began it with a touch of colic, was clearly unwell, and after bravely jumping a clear round until almost the end of the course, she faltered jumping a "double", refused at the second part of the fence, and escaped out of the ring after dumping me at the foot of the fence. We were, therefore, eliminated. Harry Llewellyn and Foxhunter went on to win the cup for the first time; and this turned out to be the last year when women were allowed to compete; the King George V event is now a Men Only affair, while women have the Queen Elizabeth Cup as part of their own White City domain. Another début, somewhat less momentous I daresay, which marked the year of that International Show, was my first broadcast with the B.B.C.

This trip to London included an historic excursion, from White City to Wembley, for the final day of the Olympic Games. No women show jumpers, of course. But here, at any rate, were men I was beginning to know well, and not only in the English team; here were great stylists such as Humberto Mariles of Mexico, winner of the Gold Medal in the Grand Prix des Nations (his horse, Arrete); and our own team headed by the great Llewellyn, with Colonel Arthur Carr and Colonel Henry Nicoll, their horses a trio of Harry Llewellyn's own mounts—Foxhunter, Monty, and Kilgeddin.

When all was over at Wembley and the White City, I said good-bye to Finality again, and returned home to Crickley to receive a new shock. We were leaving.

In spite of Mother's effort, the guest house was an intermittently prosperous business while the horses and their upkeep were a constant drain on all that we earned. At this time we had them stabled a mile or two away at the Royal George in the village of Birdlip (Crickley had only two stables); Mother proposed relinquishing the guest house for a second time and moving to the village, nearer the horses.

We rented a couple of rooms at Birdlip, where I tried pretending that being "nearer the horses" was some compensation for the loss of Crickley, but it was no good, and the forlorn feeling of emptiness reached a new depth when I was casually informed at a Show that my best boy friend had decided to marry someone else.

However, like most people, I found that the antidote for depression is hard work and there was certainly plenty of that. In addition to helping Mother with the horses I was once again doing odd jobs on local farms.

Another unfailing tonic I find is music, and though we had let Crickley furnished, Mother had taken care to have the piano installed in our living-room with the Bartlemans at Birdlip. There I practised rather more methodically than before and learnt some Beethoven and Chopin, my two favourites. Ronald, who was now working at the Ministry of Education in London, came down when he could and we were able to recapture some of the pleasure of our old musical evenings. He wrote some songs for Mother of which she was very fond.

Towards the end of the show jumping season we bought a new mare, called Carmena, and I jumped her in the Garth hunter trials, where she won an extremely good second prize of £25. She was clearly a hope for the future, but at that stage I could see neither hope nor any other satisfaction for myself, and so at the end of the summer I answered an advertisement for a job in Ireland, to which Mother agreed I should go.

With a weight on my heart and a single pound note in my purse I sailed from Fishguard at the end of October, came into Cork Harbour at seven o'clock in the morning, and caught the train north to Kilmallock, in County Limerick; fortunately I had a "through" ticket and was able to afford a light breakfast before the train departed. From the grimy carriage windows I looked out, and had to admit that the land looked good; this was my first visit to Ireland, and I began to daydream that I was hunting over the banks around me. The trouble was, despite frequent efforts to convince myself that the horse I rode was Fireworks, or the new Carmena, or a horse with any other name, the words of encouragement that I spoke aloud as the train chugged across country, were always addressed to . . . Finality. I gave the game up.

When I arrived, Kilmallock Station was cold and deserted. My new employers were late, or had forgotten I was due. I walked stamping my feet to the end of the platform, looked up at the signal box and was surprised to see the smiling Irish face of an old man watching me from the window. He turned away, threw open the door and beckoned me up the wooden stairs.

"Come up now, and let me give ye a dish o' tea," he called.

Dropping my case, I climbed the steps, warmed by his reception, half believing that it was a stairway to some sort of gnomish land above the sky, where soon I would meet face to face with the playboy of the Western World —himself.

Inside, the dear old man made me welcome, sat me on a box, gave me my tea, sweet and dark brown, and introduced himself proudly as the Station Master, though I could see no sign of other employees to do him deference. He had a small fire in his box, sat beside it sucking a black pipe of strong tobacco, and rose twice in the next half hour to switch signals for one of the few trains that came his way.

Eventually, my new employers turned up in a car, I shook hands with the old man of the Western World, and left for Rathkeale, half-an-hour's journey by road from Limerick itself, and a few miles from the waters of the Shannon.

At Rathkeale the family, a fairly wealthy one, who had engaged me, had taken over a hunting lodge. Tower Lodge. Complete with tower. Complete with small room at the top of the tower. My room. High and damp.

My first night was sleepless, not because of strange surroundings but because of the fleas—larger, fiercer, bolder fleas than I have ever known. Through the night, the beasts held an international jumping show within the darkness of the sheets, and by dawn they had crashed their fences and left their marks by the dozen on all my limbs and around my neck. I ringed the bed with DDT, but it seemed to serve no purpose beyond the novelty of an extra hurdle. Several such nights passed before the room was more or less disinfested.

My job, which lasted about a month, was varied if nothing else. I became an unusual kind of domestic help—a horse and household help. But with opportunities, nevertheless, for meeting some pleasant, interesting people, too.

My employers went hunting, and though it seemed to me that they had little experience of the sport, they appeared to enjoy it. As a rule, I would ride their horses to the meet, wherever it might be held, and there they would take over. I would then follow by car. Back at the house, my day was a full one. I laid the fires (enjoying my first experience of making a fire with peat); did some housework and some cooking; went shopping by car, acted as chauffeur for numerous other expeditions; brushed boots and cleaned the saddlery; mucked-out the stables, cleaned and helped to clip the horses. The rest of the time was my own, and one of its chief pleasures came at night, when I would slip out to the church, sit for a while, then play the organ.

At meets, and in many parts of the countryside, I made new friends, among them the great-hearted Irish character Paddy Punch, who hired out horses and was famous throughout Limerick. Then, on several days, I rode the banks with a doctor from Croome, who sallied forth to attend his cases on horseback, his instruments stuffed into the pockets of his coat or strapped to the back of the saddle; his horse, a fine hunter, was Golden Hero, bought for twelve pounds. Among my most enjoyable days was when we rode to the hill of the fairies—the celebrated landmark called Knockfierna, whose summit, they said, was haunted.

Eventually I left the tower house, counting my time as cook, parlourmaid, chauffeur, woodchopper, and stable girl as a valuable experience. A few days before my departure I was intrigued with a bustling Irish Fair in the streets of Rathkeale; the town became jammed with horses, gipsies, travelling dealers—all Irishmen, looking and living like Irishmen. They were indeed men of character.

Then, for a delightful week, I stayed in their house near the river with two of my new friends—a Dutchman, Nils Tellander, and his wife. I rode and hunted one of his horses before leaving to join Mr. and Mrs. Pat Hogan at Rathcannon. Himself a great racing jockey and trainer, Hogan taught me a good deal about jumping ditches and banks, and schooling young horses over the difficult Irish fences.

One day we went in a party to Limerick races, and on the road I observed what I took to be an agreeably reverent Irish practice. Each and every time we passed a church, the trainer, the jockeys, and all who were connected with the horses, took off their hats and solemnly rode by. A charming gesture, I thought, but one which was not repeated on the *homeward* journey when they were all in high spirits after a succesful day. That night there was a party, a wild, card-playing, noisy affair, conducted for four hours at a pace that kept me breathless, and with gambling on a scale that was quite out of my depth. It was in gay contrast to the hard work which had marked my early acquaintance with the country.

By the time I left Ireland, after an unusually merry Christmas, I felt almost restored. The visit had ended in Dublin where I had stayed with relatives, done some more riding, bought new clothes, and earned sufficient money to buy my passage home; and in the New Year I returned to Birdlip, and Mother, ready to face a jumping season which was to include my first major tour with the British team in Europe.

The first diversion of the year was the arrival of a charming little point-to-point horse called Only Just, who proceeded to win—at the long price of 12 to 1—the first race we entered. As we were led into the winner's enclosure I noticed that the crowds were scanning their programmes, puzzled, wondering what and who we were. Then, at last, the show jumping season began, and I was able to jump Carmena. Early in July, at the Royal Counties Show, Mother and I saw yet another horse which I coveted, and although our finances were still

108

in a touch-and-go condition, we decided to buy her. She was called Leona, and nine days later, at Tidworth, I jumped her for that Walwyn Challenge Cup which the great Finality had won the year before.

Leona jumped superbly; we carried off the Walwyn Cup for the second year running.

Then came the first of the Horse Shows at Harringay. Another week of happiness—Finality came back yet again. By this time Tommy Makin, for whom she had done nothing of significance, had sold Final to Mr. and Mrs. Snodgrass, who lived near Edinburgh, and it was for them I jumped her at Harringay. And although I had not seen or ridden Final for many months, we slipped easily into our familiar pattern of understanding. At Harringay she excelled herself and won the competition for the leading show jumper of the year.

Again I was invited to join the British team, this time for an important Continental tour of shows in Paris, Brussels, Zurich, and Geneva. I was doubly satisfied, for the Snodgrasses had promised that I could take Finality, my own horse for the tour being Leona.

Long ago accustomed to last-minute calamities and disappointments, I was not even surprised when, a few hours before the horses were due to sail, Mr. Snodgrass telephoned to announce that although he appreciated the importance of Finality's inclusion in the British team for an international tour, nevertheless he would prefer her to stay home so that his son could jump her in one of the hunter trials to be held near their Scottish home. Later, I learned that Final had indeed been entered for this local contest in Scotland, but that she was, unfortunately, beaten. It could hardly have been more of a disappointment—the sort of heartbreak that always seemed to happen to me and Final.

The last-minute change of plans did, of course, succeed in upsetting my arrangements, and I feared that I would be stuck with only one horse—almost a novice, as Leona was—to take abroad. But my friend Mary Whitehead, who was off on a hunting trip to Ireland, came to the rescue with the loan of her fine horse, Nobbler, who was at once despatched to Paris. He had been brought up from grass, was not particularly fit, and even his shoes had been fitted while on the way to the boat; added to this, I had never jumped him, and so I had few hopes for our success abroad.

When the shows began, Leona the "novice" and Nobbler the "unfit" proceeded to give me the surprise of my life. First in Paris. Here, Leona turned up trumps and won the Prix de Diane, which was, as I told her, not bad for her first trip overseas. Nobbler had puffed his way through the Paris events without success; but every hour we got a little more used to each other, and every day he became a good deal fitter.

On to Brussels. Nobbler astonished the entire team, and I think himself, by pulling off nothing less than the Grand Prix. This consisted of three competitions, with difficult courses, and it was a sensational achievement for him. He won the doubles and trebles competition, and was sufficiently well-placed in other events to gather up enough points for victory in the final placing. I had been especially impressed by his performance over a narrow double fence, with not a single stride in between the two obstacles; you merely jumped the first fence, landed, took off without a pause, and jumped the second. No easy task, but Nobbler went like a stag.

Then to Zurich. I drove there in the company of Harry Llewellyn and his wife, Teeny, who were now comparatively old friends. The first stages of this journey tended to be, for Teeny and me, little more than an informative lesson in strategic warfare as soon as we began driving across the battlefields over which Harry had fought.

Every so often, Harry would pull up, leap from the car, and race away, telling us as he departed:

"Most interesting. Shan't be long. *Must* go up this hill and find out how much the German tanks were able to see."

He would return, satisfied, after ten minutes, and drive on—until the next battle memory hove in sight.

For the events at Zurich and Geneva I rode only Leona, who went extremely well; in Geneva, especially, she jumped with brilliance and was placed in every event. It was altogether an enjoyable show in which, for women contestants, Leona achieved the most consistent results, thereby providing me with an award which became my most prized mantelpiece decoration: a superbly-designed gold-plated clock which was set inside a heavy stirrup, the clock hands embellished with miniature horseshoes.

The days of our homeward journey to England included my twenty-first birthday. We drove from Geneva, through the country where the Rhône cuts the mountains and the deep green colours seem to be impossible; then up the great rocks and over the Juras.

Here, on the highest, loneliest, and loveliest col, the car broke down.

With Harry at the wheel, for the path was treacherous,

Teeny and I pushed the car two hundred yards to a rise that overlooked a small farm far below. Then we free-wheeled kilometres down the mountain, hoping for the best. At the foot, the road levelled out; we began laying bets on how far we could travel, but the car surprised us all by trickling steadily to a full stop within a yard of the farm walls.

We went inside, not very hopeful about the prospect of finding help in this remote backwater. The young man who came out to examine the engine was a German ex-prisoner of war, a rural worker who said little and looked as unlike a skilled mechanic as Teeny or I.

Suddenly he asked for a hairpin, which we gave him, doubtfully. Within an hour we were on our way, heading for Paris, and humbled by the easy skill with which the silent young man had solved our engine problems.

After a night in Châlon-sur-Saône, where we enjoyed a vast French dinner, we reached Paris on the morning of my twenty-first. I was given a magnificent party by the Comte de Maillé and his wife, who were old friends; and with Harry and Teeny I paid my first visit to the Folies Bergère, where that great artist Josephine Baker was reducing audiences to tears with a fine performance as Mary Queen of Scots.

But perhaps the most diverting experience that France had to offer me, then or at any other time, was my drag hunt day at Chesney, which resembled more than anything else a comedy on the scale that only the inimitable French film can usually achieve. Our host was Jean de Beaumont, who lived at Chesney, which lay not far from Orleans. He had not only invited us to take part in the drag hunt, but had seemed to advertise the fact

With Harry Llewellyn, Wilfred White and Peter Robeson after winning the Prince of Wales Cup at the White City in 1952. *L. to R.:* Tosca, Foxhunter, Nizefela, Craven A

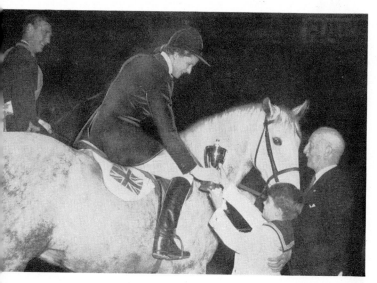

Receiving the cup for the 1952 Grand Prix at Brussels from Prince Alexander. Our good friend Comte Roland de Maillé, wearing the sash of the Leading Rider, was second

If Monty had cleared this fence in Algiers he would have won the
£200 championship. The far pole toppled off well after he had
landed. Such is the luck of the game

Tosca's awful fall over a bank at Nice. This was my first and last
appearance at the Show that week

(*Above*) Tosca
after winning the
Coronation Cup
at the Richmond
Royal Horse
Show, 1953

(*Right*) Tosca
turning while
jumping during a
speed competition
at the Bath and
West Show, 1953

Jumping for the Athlone Cup at Blackpool on Prince Hal

White City, 1953. Col. Ansell presents me with my rosette as the winner of the Ladies' Débutante Jumping Competition on Prince Hal

over the whole of France, judging by the streams of foot travellers who attended. I was told that these spectators numbered four thousand, and it was clear from the start that the attitude of some of them was to come and view the English show jumpers make idiots of themselves.

We were mounted on green and uncontrollable army horses from Fontainebleau, an assembly of rakish creatures who appeared never in their lives to have seen, much less followed, hounds. Most of the horses were equipped with rusty snaffles and reins like stiff cardboard. When they saw the hounds they went wild with excitement.

Harry, who had survived a number of far-from-simple Grand Nationals at home, was forced to abandon his horse, saying it was the most dangerous animal he had ever encountered. Mine was considerably less menacing, though no less comic, and away we went in a cloud of dust; after the first two riders had departed it was almost impossible for the rest of us to see for the dust, and I know that one fashionably-garbed pair rode off in the wrong direction.

The rest of the facts seem even to me to be ludicrous exaggerations; but I must set them down as they happened.

For one thing, most of us were virtually run away with by our horses, for they galloped gazing at the sky, and although the ditches and fences were so small as to be of no consequence, they became a dangerous hazard when your horse insisted on gazing fixedly at the heavens. Every few minutes there would be a check, when small groups equipped with hunting horns would blow the appropriate call. Everyone stopped, and there was an

113

interval for drinks. Then off we all went once more—flat out—the expert riders among the men as helpless on their mounts as the elegant women who rode side-saddle.

After we had started hunting, I was puzzled to observe that our numbers seemed oddly depleted. I found the answer as I approached a clump of trees, into which a young and handsome rider, now dismounted, was gallantly leading his partner, and as I passed them by I saw that they were locked in a fond embrace.

Meanwhile, the crowds of lookers-on had somehow stayed with us, thronging the path of the hunt as if they were watching a point-to-point race, and hoping for spills. Approaching a ditch, which I jumped, I was astonished to hear an excited French voice wafting across from the trees—delivering a racy commentary through a microphone and loudspeaker.

"Voilà Mademoiselle Pat Smythe! L'Anglaise! Elle approche! Elle saute! Attention! Elle tombe! Hélas! Mais non, attendez, elle ne tombe pas!"

And, helpless with laughter, I almost did fall off.

Teeny Llewellyn was riding with me, and a moment later we stopped as Teeny observed the fall from her horse of an elegant French lady, who screamed, and then lay still. A quartet of men immediately turned and galloped to her aid.

Teeny and I also went back to give her some help. But when we arrived the unfortunate lady was not at all pleased to see us—we were altogether unwanted, for she was lying there, all but stripped to the waist, while four men bent over her murmuring words of comfort and kissing her hands and cheeks. Five minutes later, bored with this charade, they galloped away, leaving the poor woman—who had in fact broken a wrist—to her fate.

By the time the hunt was over, Teeny and I were dishevelled and grimy. But from out of the trees came a steady stream of couples leading their horses, elegant as when the day had started. The various groups with their hunting horns brought the stragglers together with delicate, musical calls, answering each other across the trees, and the performance ended when a stag—killed the day before—was dragged triumphantly to the "Finish" and thrown to the hounds.

Drinks were again provided, and the atmosphere took on the character of a cocktail party. After that, we were ushered into the château and told to change for dinner. Clearly we were not meant to be in need of a wash for there was no hot water. The lights fused, so men and women had to change in the same room by the light of two candles. But it was worth it, for there followed quite the most brilliant banquet and ball I have ever attended. The party ended characteristically the following morning when our host courteously awoke each of the ladies —with a delicate embrace.

Such was my introduction to international sport. I had enjoyed it, but was quite ready to return home.

CHAPTER 7

ENTER PRINCE HAL

AND home now meant—Miserden.

Here, in a Cotswold wood by a castle lake, Edward the Black Prince had courted his Fair Maid of Kent, presumably in the late fifties of the fourteenth century, since the lady married him in 1361. But by the winter of 1949, when Mother and I moved in, the British Army had added its own inimitable markings to those of the centuries.

About Miserden, a village of simple beauty a few miles from our old home at Crickley, there is an ancient manorial air. It was to the old Dower House of the great estate (thanks to Wing Commander and Mrs. Huntley Sinclair) that Mother and I came to set up what we hoped would turn into a bigger, better, and more beautiful guest house, near to a rented field which, with the aid of tree trunks and old petrol drums, would become my makeshift training quarters for the life of show jumping. The grey stone dower house and its stables lay near the end of the twisting village road; away to our right were the gates of the estate and its hidden lake among the wooded hills; in front we looked out across country, surveying three peaceful valleys. On the first evening, Mother and I stood watching the sun go down, and she spoke softly:

"Aren't we lucky to be here—it's wonderful to have a home again."

I put my arm round her for I knew what this meant to her and we went back to the house to finish the painting, scrubbing, hanging of curtains, and laying of carpets. We put final dabs of paint on the woodwork of the stone-floored hallway at four o'clock one crisp December morning and shook hands with the first guests of our house-warming Christmas party at four o'clock in the afternoon of the same day. We were, as the saying goes, tired but very happy.

A few weeks later arrived our first guest from the Continent—my friend Michele Cancre, aged nineteen, who had been my show jumping rival for three years since the days of my first British-team expedition to Ostend and Le Zoute; she was engaged to the celebrated D'Orgeix, whom I had first seen in the Olympic Games, and later they married. On this visit to Miserden, Michele was delighted to see English hunting, and I took her several times out with different packs, in particular the Cotswold and the Beaufort hounds.

In the spring of 1950 I went racing at Cheltenham—that is, as a spectator, and, as always, as cheaply as possible. My method cost me nothing. I could neither afford, nor did I especially wish for, the twenty-shilling entrances or the owners' enclosure; and for me it would be a sport to watch out on the course—no charge for this—along with thousands of others. On the day of the Kim Muir Steeplechase I found a fine position beside the last fence and, while I waited, discussed the prospects for the Gold Cup, a day or so later, with a stocky expert Irishman who reminded me of that Station Master of

Kilmallock who had welcomed me with tea in his signal-box.

Then the 'chase began, and from the start there were many falls; even Mighty Fine, who might have won, slipped on the flat and was out of the race. Only a few horses were left running by the time the last fence was reached. But suddenly I observed a superb jump over the fence by a handsome-looking chestnut, who plodded up the hill to come in third, not actually a remarkable achievement because most of the better horses had fallen.

A few hours later I met Kilpatrick, the trainer, and learned that the horse called Fourtowns, whose jump had so impressed me, was to be sold; it seemed that an old trouble with a tendon meant he was no longer fast enough for racing. The price was only £150. Next day Mother and I drove over to Collingbourne Ducis to see the Kilpatrick horses; a misty dull rain was blowing across the downs when Fourtowns was brought out of his stable for my inspection. He was full of beans as he jiggled in the yard, and though the drizzle dripped on my neck I fell in love with him because he was such a fine-looking, princely horse. They put up a racing saddle and told me to go and try him over the steeplechase jumps, which I did; and quickly I saw that he had much to learn, for he jumped very "big", dragged his hind legs and pulled like a train. But there were no doubts that I still wanted him, so I paid, with Mother's co-operation, the £150 and brought him home to Miserden.

His name, Fourtowns, troubled me. Whatever sentimental or social significance it may have possessed for others, to me it was empty, flat, and thoroughly unmemorable; in fact it referred to the village in Ireland where he had been bred. To me it was ugly for such a good-looking horse. But what to put in its place? Then my thoughts went back to a scene, a few nights earlier, when I had gone alone to the cinema to see for the fifth time Laurence Olivier's film *Henry the Fifth*. Always one of my favourite Shakespeare plays, I thought also of my favourite passage in it, and pictured Olivier, the young warrior, tensely building the courage of his men during the Battle of Agincourt . . .

> "I see you stand like greyhounds in the slips,
> Straining upon the start. The game's afoot;
> Follow your spirit, and upon this charge
> Cry—God for Harry! England! and Saint George!"

That settled it. Fourtowns became Prince Hal, and I made a mental note that if I ever got the chance I would thank Mr. Olivier—who was not then Sir Laurence—for the inspired tip.

If the change of name brought a certain satisfaction, then the first outing with Prince Hal filled me no less with a strong foreboding of disappointment. I feared, indeed, that I had made an abominable blunder in buying him. He was a racehorse who could only jiggle sideways; he could not walk straight; he wanted mainly to gallop; he would not circle; he was excessively nervous even for a thoroughbred. As I tried vainly to canter him in a small circle—which is the sole method of acquiring control—the cries of children at play in the village school were enough to bring him out in a lather from head to foot. The slightest sound became a nervy distraction, a reminder, to Hal, of the noisy racecourse—

but with no race to follow. He was extremely one-sided, unable to turn in both directions; in fact, his backbone would bend only one way, and when I tried to turn him the other, he flatly refused all co-operation. The task seemed hopeless, and the prospect of turning him into a show jumper, laughable. Except that I couldn't afford hopelessness. Not at £150.

In a few days, fortunately for both of us, the situation improved. I managed to get Prince Hal working, though not at a very collected pace, which was hardly surprising since he'd never been collected in his life. But there remained the problem of his unbalance, and after another week of effort I was still desperate about his unwillingness to bend his backbone.

Then, one morning, I had an idea. I went out to his stable where, after a few minutes of what I hoped was soothing talk, I moved buckets and obstacles out of his path, distributed half a bale of straw around the stable, selected a thin rope . . . and tied his head to his tail, bending him from left to right.

I got out just in time, for Hal went berserk, whirled furiously around in tight little circles, broke out in a lather, and fought bravely but impotently against the constricting rope which bent him in the direction he did not want to bend. After an exhausting struggle he gave up trying, stood sweating but still, and gazed in bewilderment at his tied-up tail from out of the corner of his right eye.

For one hour I left him to reflect on Woman's inhumanity to Man, then returned, untied him, put on his saddle and bridle, and took him out to the field. He went like a lamb, turning in either direction and responding to all my aids and encouragement as if there had never been a sign of discord.

Not that this victory meant the end of our training troubles. Prince Hal clearly loved jumping, but in steeplechasing fashion, and I found it necessary from time to time to let him pretend that we were "off to the races". But the main task was to cure him of precisely that illusion, and so, rather than let him take his fences in straight line, I began jumping him in a circle. This gave me much more control, and after a few days he began concentrating on the jump rather than on using his spring when he landed as a means of galloping away at forty miles an hour. I learned, too, that he hated touching his fences; always over-sensitive, he became quite upset whenever he scraped the top, and soon I began watching his "geste"—the movement and folding of his legs while jumping. This problem of "geste" was important. Hal had a huge *natural* jumping ability, and was accustomed to taking-off a long way from the fence, jumping high and clear, without troubling to fold his legs. One afternoon, alone in a field, I dismounted, and while Hal looked on with what seemed a pitying expression, I pretended to deliver him a classroom lecture, saying, so far as I recall:

"When the forelegs leave the ground, they should fold up . . ."

Hal began to look bored . . .

". . . so that your knees are brought up to your chin . . ."

Now he whinneyed, but turned his head away . . .

"and if you fold them properly, your body will not have to go so high in order to clear the fence . . ."

Hal gave me a sidelong glance.

121

". . . and all this dangling of your legs over a jump is probably no more than over-anxiety . . ."

Hal chewed at a tuft of grass; he had never looked less anxious.

". . . so perhaps we could try it again, keeping as calm as possible."

And Hal tried it again.

And again. And again. Experience was what he needed, and what he received; with it, his "geste" began to show clear signs of improvement.

At Whitsun I took him to his first show, and the only mistake, perhaps, was its location; for the show was held at Bishop's Cleeve, right on the site of his last race a few months earlier; there was the old familiar scene, with Cleeve Hill in the background and the scent of the race-course under his nose. This time, he thought, he was *really* off to the races.

When I started him in the jumping I did not have much control; we went round at full speed, and as we approached one gate it blew slightly in the wind, causing Hal to swerve. He jumped straight over the wing of the gate, five feet and a bit, and I marvelled that he even landed safely. Then we came to the water jump, sailed across it, and I had to use every ounce of strength I possessed to pull him up from a gallop which he obviously assumed was part of a four-mile steeplechase.

Throughout the summer, aside from bringing Prince Hal to that pitch of confidence, and competence, which would take him into the ring at more important show jumping competitions, I went on jumping Carmena and Leona, until the White City Show brought the "jinx" which I had now come to accept as an annual misfortune.

This time Leona, for whom I had good hopes, fell ill, and I entered the White City events only with Carmena, who jumped well, though without any major successes.

Hal got his chance as early as August when I entered him for the important international trials held at Weston-super-Mare. I was also to jump Carmena and Leona in these events.

When the jumping began, all my hopes for Prince Hal were raised, for he went superbly, beat both Carmena and Leona, as well as other fine horses, and won his first international trial, as pleased with his performance as I was with the £40 prize cheque it added to my still slender balance at the bank.

With September came the yearly delight of meeting an old friend; another reunion with the great Finality. I was to jump her once again, in the Horse of the Year Show at Harringay, for the Snodgrasses, and, as always, she greeted me with her customary joyful push in the stomach, and performed for me with more than customary brilliance. Carmena and Leona also went well, and were placed in several events; in a sense, I felt occasionally mean-spirited where Carmena was concerned, for although she won me a great deal I could never lavish any love upon her. And I knew why. Carmena had arrived when Finality was first lost to me, and in those days I had cared for nothing, even believing that I did not want to own another horse, so powerful was my attachment to Final; as a consequence, Carmena got the blunt end of my bitterness.

Finality's swan song was played in that Horse of the Year Show; this was her night if ever she knew one—the night of the Fred Foster test competition. The night

123

of my duel with Colonel Harry Llewellyn, of Final's duel with the magnificent Foxhunter. The night when the television cameras helped to bring the fascination and thrills of show jumping into millions of homes where show jumping was no more than a name, where several thousand new enthusiasts for the sport were created inside a single hour.

Llewellyn and Foxhunter had been going exceptionally well, and at one stage it seemed certain, so smooth and pure was Foxhunter's display, that the victory would be theirs. Final, nevertheless, was equally inspired, and as the tension grew and the crowds became more hushed with suppressed excitement, I realized that she was truly in the mood that makes for faultless jumping. Higher and higher went the fences. Foxhunter cleared them all; but so did Finality. Higher still; and still they went on brilliantly. Jump-off followed jump-off, and I wondered how and when it would end. The roof of my mouth became dry, I longed for a drink, licked the damp from my upper lip, felt certain my lipstick was smeared, and knew that my nose was shining. I glanced across at Harry Llewellyn, who smiled, set his jaw, and rode into the last stages of the battle.

The final jump-off included a high wall with a pole on top, and I made our approach confidently but with extra care. Finality was so small that spectators on the far side of the fence could not even see her coming, and their first glimpse of her was at the moment of our take-off. She jumped—high and well, but a fraction too low to clear the pole, which toppled lightly into the dirt. Four faults, and the great Foxhunter also had four faults. So, after an hour's jumping, the contest was called off and the result declared a tie. We were equal firsts with no less than Llewellyn himself—and his Foxhunter. I remembered my first sight of the Colonel in action at a White City show where I had been an unhappy school-girl spectator; it seemed like a lifetime ago; it was, in fact, just four years.

After the Harringay duel, Finality went back to Scotland, and the men of the British team went off to America —Llewellyn, White, and Peter Robeson. But another British team was chosen for the international show in Paris that autumn, and when I was selected for this trip I asked Harry Llewellyn what I might do about a partner for Leona. Characteristically generous, he offered me that wonderful horse Kilgeddin, and I set off for Paris.

Bad news awaited me in France. I had dispatched the horses a day earlier, and tragedy had struck Leona on the journey. While the train was standing at a station, she had been badly kicked by another horse, had backed up inside the box and fallen through the open door, between the platform and the train. After frantic efforts Leona was extricated and calmed, but one of her legs was gashed.

Even Kilgeddin was not entirely sound, but by the day of the show both horses were sufficiently patched up to be ready for jumping, and we entered the fray keeping our fingers, so to speak, doubly crossed.

It occurred to me later that horses, perhaps, are like Englishmen—at their best with backs to the wall; at any rate, the analogy seemed to hold good for our English horses, and in particular for old Kilgeddin, who calmly knocked aside the supposed supremacy of the French and the Spaniards. A few years before, the British show jumping team had been derisively scorned by experienced Continentals. During this memorable Parisian October, they became less sure; perhaps they had guessed that throughout those years we had watched our rivals closely, had learned from those who had smiled indulgently the tricks of jumping large spread fences, jumping at speed, cutting out corners to save split seconds, and turning ourselves into a force to be reckoned with.

The atmosphere in the Vel D'Hiver made us thoroughly uncomfortable; it was hot and sticky, and the ground was covered in deep layers of black dirt. Galloping down to the high jump, galloping fast as one must in order to achieve the required impetus, the black dust filled our eyes, mouths and nostrils and generally created the worst possible conditions for good jumping.

But Kilgeddin, scorning the difficulties, cleared 6 feet $10\frac{7}{8}$ inches, and made it with ease.

We were not asked to try jumping higher, since no other rider had cleared the fence at all, and Kilgeddin's great effort set up a European record for women riders. Aside from this high jump championship Kilgeddin also won the Coupe Dubonnet, and together with Leona's creditable display, helped to achieve for me the distinction of being declared the best woman performer throughout the show; at the time I felt considerably flattered, though as the years pass I become ever more convinced that honours in show jumping are more aptly pinned to the horse than to the rider.

Before leaving France I celebrated our victories by buying from my friend Michele Cancre a fine little Anglo-Arab stallion called Djort; he was a *petit* chestnut with a free and lovely action, who seemed to carry himself with a distinctly French, indeed a decidedly Parisian air.

On that day, too, I had been presented to the Duke and Duchess of Windsor, and reminded the Duke that on the battlefields of France during the First World War, a certain young army officer had been associated with him—Captain Eric Smythe, my father.

Then the Duchess invited me to dine with them. We went to a small, exclusive night club in Montmartre where I was intrigued to sit by while the ex-King of England was gently "ticked off" by his wife for fiddling with the cutlery on the restaurant table. Every now and then I experienced a mild surprise when I heard him addressed as "David"—absurdly half expecting that even his wife might refer to "His Royal Highness".

The Duke and Duchess had watched the jumping that day, and we mostly talked horses. They were interested to know what the ground had been like, and the Duchess especially had observed the difficult conditions. She plied me with questions: had it not been excessively dirty? Was it impossible to see with all the flying dust? And had the dust harmed the horses' eyes? Sipping our wine, we recalled, too, the amazing performance of the Spahi horsemen from Morocco, who had given an exhibition of equestrian acrobatics on a scale that was rare even in the circus ring.

Another royal personage—the Sultan of Morocco—had been rather less pleased. During the exhibition, the Sultan watched his mounted subjects winning the applause of the show jumping world, and had looked thoroughly satisfied until the moment of their grand climax. This was a dramatic charge of horsemen at full speed

—fifty to sixty robed riders on magnificent bay and grey stallions, each movement carried out to a piercing whistle command.

Just before the charge came an impressive cartwheel pattern of riding, with the Spahis in flowing robes, standing gracefully on their saddles—I looked across at the benign, bearded Sultan, who was smiling in anticipation.

Suddenly, without warning, the horses anticipated the whistle, broke into a mad gallop, threw half the brave Spahis into the dust and careered all over the ring in uproar and chaos.

I looked again at the Sultan. The smile had gone, and a dark glower was on his face.

Tosca clearing the water at the White City, 1953

Tosca jumping the last fence in the Prince of Wales Cup

Taking the water jump with Prince Hal at the White City, 195?

After winning the Prince of Wales Cup in 1953 each member of
the team receives a silver salver from the Duke of Beaufort

CHAPTER 8

TOSCA, HAL, AND ROMANTIC
DISILLUSION

THEN came Tosca, the deceptively placid-looking grey mare whose show jumping victories within the next two years were to average one a week. Like Prince Hal she was a bargain at £150, but there the comparison ended.

Tosca had arrived during the hunting season, and I took her out frequently with the Cotswold and the Beaufort packs. Wildly impatient, often uncontrollable, and with a disconcerting habit of "fly bucking" whenever she reached a fence, she had to learn the hard way. I would therefore hack her to the meets, making her sufficiently tired to be able to control her while hunting, then hack her home again at night. Next day, just for good measure and to ensure that she did not get above herself, I would give her two hours' "dressage"—that systematic work which makes a horse quiet, supple, and obedient, so that, in the language of textbook training, "he becomes pleasant in his movements and comfortable for his rider".

She may or may not have derived "pleasure" from her movements; but what is certain is that she gave little or no comfort to her rider, and on more than one occasion I was in grave danger of being tossed into the solid bulk of a Cotswold stone wall. My hunting with Tosca was interrupted, however, when I was put out of action in the New Year of 1951 by an enforced visit to hospital—for a minor operation.

No riding for six weeks, an order which irked me considerably at the start of what was to become the busiest show jumping year of my life thus far.

At this time Mother and I were entertaining a young Swiss friend called Sam Koechlin, a tall, curly-haired law student from Basle, who seemed to live largely on grapefruit and black coffee when he was not in London pursuing his studies for a law degree.

Sam often came to Miserden for week-ends, to get what he called "a little bit of fresh airs and riding". From Switzerland he had sent to us his own horse so that once a week he could ride and train for the Badminton three-day event in which he wanted to compete. Not only a jumper of some prowess, Sam was also an expert in the arts of dressage, and from him I learned a good deal about how I should work the excitable Tosca. When the doctor announced that for the remainder of January I should be confined to bed, I was somewhat concerned over Tosca's progress. About her ultimate future as a show jumper of exceptional brilliance I had no doubts, despite the teething troubles, and I knew that like Hal in *his* tempestuous early days she loved her jumping.

But what to do during these six weeks of idleness? Suddenly I remembered Sam, who was arriving that night.

"Would you like to ride Tosca for me while I am away?" I asked him at breakfast next day.

Sam was delighted. "I would be incredibly happy about it," he said, with the extravagance that went with his pleasant accent and unusually charming manners.

"Are there some special requirements?" he went on.

"Yes, as a matter of fact," I told him, "there are. I want you to take her hunting, and to jump her over gates. That is what she badly needs."

"It will be a pleasure," said Sam.

"Please don't forget the gates, Sam," I urged. "It's really most important. Jump her over every gate in the county if you've got the energy." And I went to pack my bag for an unwanted "holiday" in my semi-private ward.

The events of the next fortnight reached me in several versions, one being Sam's, another the more sober analysis of a mutual friend. Piece by piece, however, the story emerged, and I was able to build an accurate picture of Sam's well-meant though sometimes misunderstood gallantry among the English ladies on horseback.

Sam, I learned, had taken to heart my instructions concerning Tosca and gates; had indeed taken them almost literally. Out hunting one day, he set off in the company of a well-groomed lady who had a certain timidity about jumping. The conversation and the horses proceeded at an amiable trot until, in one field, they came to a gate in the wall. Sam—a gracious compliment ready, as it were, on his lips for the moment she had jumped it—was surprised to hear instead the cultured English voice asking:

"Would you be so kind as to open the gate?"

A trifle puzzled by this new concept of hunting *sans* jumping, Sam nevertheless leaped from Tosca's back, opened wide the gate and, ever the gentleman, raised his hat with a smile as the lady trotted regally into the field beyond. Sam caught an answering smile of gratitude as she pulled up to wait for him.

Gratitude, however, turned to fury when she saw what happened. Sam carefully closed the gate, rode Tosca back a few yards, turned, put her into a gallop and jumped her into the second field to rejoin the now pink-cheeked huntress.

When the hunt ended, Sam discussed the incident with one of the men in the party as they stood over a whisky.

"Good heavens, old boy, that was a terrible insult to the lady. What on earth made you do such a thing?"

Sam, hopelessly bewildered, shook his head. "Miss Smythe told me to jump Tosca over every gate in the county—I must not miss one. And that was a gate, my friend, so I jumped it. But I opened it for the lady to pass through—that is good manners, yes? Then I closed it—that is correct, yes? I do not see any insult."

When I returned home, Mother and I were regaled yet again with Sam's tale of Tosca, The Lady, and the Gate. But when he concluded, we decided there was little prospect of helping him to grasp the cloudy enigmas of hunting etiquette.

The second example of Sam's conscientious determination to put Tosca across every gate in sight gave him no more than an undignified fall and a two-mile trek home—on foot. I had returned from hospital to my bedroom at Miserden and was roused from a book by the sound of Tosca's hooves clattering on the stones outside. I looked up, and saw she was riderless. Sam returned alone half an hour later to explain, ruefully, that the mare had made it painfully clear she did not intend jumping one of his chosen gates. "I'm afraid she stopped rather suddenly—and I jumped it alone," grinned Sam. Tosca, at all events, had found her own way home, across fields and main roads, and although she was unharmed, she has never since been comfortable within earshot of traffic.

Free at last from medical orders, I got back to work and soon found that Tosca was a wonderful hunter to take across country, although always she gave too much of herself in the daytime and paid for it by sweating through the night from excitement. When spring came she started jumping the fences we made from rustic pine poles balanced on old tins and oil drums—often poached, I fear, from . . . well, anyway, often poached.

During the first few days, I was depressed by her treatment of these fences, for she revealed what seemed like an obsessional caution, and either wanted to jump them high and clear, or not at all; this desire gave her a strong preference for taking-off close to the fence, in order to go high over the top, and I realized that great care was needed. Above all, I told myself I must show no sign of over-anxiety, since if a rider gets too cautious the horse will certainly follow suit; so I made a practice of never asking her to take-off too far away, in case she lost confidence and refused the fence. When the ground became harder, a new and terrible fear entered Tosca's heart: a horror at finding sand or peat on the far side of a fence (to prevent jarring a horse's legs). For some reason she loathed treading on them, and if she glimpsed sand or peat while in mid-air she would leap far forward, trying desperately to clear them—and often landing with her hind legs first.

Yet from Tosca I learned so much. One spring evening, a group of children from the nearby school sat on the wall of our paddock watching Tosca at work. As the noise of their chatter drifted across the stubble I reflected that horses, like children, must be guided with love and patience into the right paths; that like children they were quick to take advantage of difficult situations; and that, unlike many children, they have exceedingly good memories, so that one must be ready at all times to counter any preconceived notions while giving them a fair indication of one's intentions. I thought of a rider I had seen in the show ring the year before, losing her temper with a horse after a poor display. The jumping faults had clearly been the rider's, and I had been furious at the sight of her unjust punishment of her mount. With Tosca, especially, I saw the pitfalls that lay ahead if I acted without intelligence, and I determined that Tosca should become, so far as it lay in my power, a model of good "schooling" in every sense of the word.

In time, Tosca became less nervy, more amenable to the constant schooling I gave her in small circles at a slow trot, and less suspicious of the fences and obstacles of the show ring. Her first shows, indeed, brought bounding confidence, and in April I entered her for the Western Counties jumping competitions—together with Prince Hal, who was now a veritable Adonis among jumpers. The weather for this show was appalling, with rain, hail, thunder, and heavy going. Tosca went well but was unplaced. Hal, on the other hand, jumped brilliantly despite the mud, and seemed unable to make a false step. On his performance that week he was selected to join the

British show jumping team, bound for Madrid in May—although he had never yet performed at an international show in England.

The party for Madrid consisted of Harry and Teeny Llewellyn, Ruby Holland-Martin, Michael Webber, and me. First we went by air to Nice, where Harry and Ruby had left their cars (having returned earlier from Italy). From Nice, Harry drove his own car, while I followed with Ruby's old but powerful Bentley.

We covered a thousand miles from the far end of the French Riviera to the centre of Madrid in just two days, passing the first night at the strange ghostly city of Les Baux, in the Rhône Valley, and the second on the Costa Brava, just north of Barcelona. We were intrigued, in Spain that morning, to observe the Spaniards' reaction to a drizzle of rain. In London, a million office-bound workers would have hurried through the streets without comment; but during May in Barcelona the rain was almost a sensation, and the roads were filled with cycling workers carrying umbrellas.

Along the rough country roads to Madrid I looked at the red earth where sparsely scattered scrub vegetation made odd green patches; saw small boys, dressed only in blankets, herding goats, happy, but ill-nourished; saw oxen ploughing the peasant land with only a stick behind them—literally scratching the earth after the fashion of stone-age farming; on land such as this, I thought, the blades of corn must be yards apart, and I wondered how in the world a man and his family contrived to live: their houses were hovels built against the sides of the hills, mere holes in the walls for windows and doors. And the ravages of the civil war were still to be seen.

We lunched at five in the afternoon, but by this time we were too exhausted to appreciate that this was, in fact, the right time for the meal in sunny Spain. Eventually we reached Madrid where we put up at the Hotel Florida.

Early next morning I went out to see Prince Hal, who had been shipped across several days before. An immediate shock. Hal had developed a swelling on his back, caused by a warble fly; it was already a painful spot for the poor horse, and only by cutting a hole in the saddle pad was it possible to ride him.

When the Madrid show got under way, Prince Hal displayed a wonderful resilience considering that he was jumping in his first international competition with the disability of a poisoned back. For me, an entirely new experience was the gambling on our performances; substantial betting, on each section of the competition, slowed up the jumping considerably, but since nothing was ever hurried in Spain, and the sun beat down throughout the day, no one worried. The Spanish family who entertained me to lunch one day came to the show in the evening, put a few pesetas on Prince Hal, and were delighted when he won the jumping in his section, the "tote" paying out at a high price.

My own delight lay in the frequent excursions we made during the intervals of the show. The day of Corpus Christi, for example, was a rest day which we spent at Toledo, the capital of old Spain where El Greco had lived and painted some of his vividly majestic works. Here we watched the great procession of Corpus Christi, hundreds of white-robed children in slow, serious march to their first communion, with the Madonna carried high amid the banners, the fancy dress, the gipsy carts, the bicycles, and the people jamming Toledo's narrow streets. It was a bizarre mixture of glad rags and holiness, ending in the big noisy plaza with a fiesta bullfight where they brought not merely the usual three matadors and six bulls, but "four matadors, senorita . . . *four* matadors and *eight* bulls."

This, however, was a less superb *corrida*, a less polished bullfighting festival than the brave, brilliant display I saw in Madrid. Nothing is worse, or looks more cruel, or less entertaining, than a *bad* bullfight. The bad fight with much blood and no art is truly a disgusting sight. But the good fight, the brave fight, with brave bulls and matadors inspired—such as we saw in the *corrida* at Madrid—that is a ballet with death, where danger blends with grace, and where the sword is a dancing point to be used only as the last flourish in a movement of finesse. On that day I saw the sport at its best as I watched a brilliant performance by the celebrated Antonio Ordonez who triumphed with three "ears" and a tail, the symbols of his grace and bravery. As the crowds streamed from the plaza, I wondered what it would be like to be there in the ring, hearing the cheers —or the muttered grumbles, as the case may be—out there alone with a cape in hand and a brave bull to face. . . .

I went back to the hotel, unfolded my bath towel and —using the bed-posts for my bull—made charging "passes", "veronicas", and other intricate matador movements until an astonished team mate looked in at the door to call me away for a cocktail.

Before starting the jumping another day I walked into the Prado to drink the glories of a few more El Grecos;

the weird, nightmare pictures by Goya gave me a fascinated horror, and the Velasquez paintings of horses much simple joy.

Then to the show, where the great-hearted Prince Hal jumped his way to victory in the *Prueba Amazones*, or, to give the English title, the Ladies' Competition—but how much finer it looks and sounds in Spanish. Adding to the team's achievement, Teeny Llewellyn came second on Foxhunter. Next day, although the tender spot on his back had grown a little worse, Hal jumped brilliantly once again, and in the contest for the Grand Prix he touched just one fence; in the final placing he was the top British horse.

On another rest day we journeyed to El Escorial where we toured the sombre palace in the shadows of the Guadarrama Mountains. In this summer palace of former Spanish kings we were shown the gloomy room where Philip II died of melancholia. I could well believe it.

By this time, we of the British team had become nicely accustomed to the notion that apart from our jumping life in Spain should be regarded largely as a time of siesta and sightseeing, dancing and dining—and then more siesta. You can never be late in Spain, they said, because we lunch at five o'clock and dine at midnight. Nobody could be late in Spain . . . except the British team, though I cannot to this day imagine how or why it was that we contrived to be the last arrivals at every party we attended, whether private and cheerful with a family of new Spanish friends, or noisy and public and lasting far into the night at such places as the Villa Rosa, or the old smugglers' den of Las Cuevas de Luis Chandelas where I became fascinated by the Flamencan singers, dancers, and music from guitars.

One night's show jumping took place almost in darkness, but it was a good night for Britain. Ruby Holland-Martin had flown to Madrid, to collect, among other things, his car which I had raced from Nice. Ruby also collected the important puissance competition, riding the discovery of the British team, a horse called Aherlow.

Among the fences in one contest were double banks—where you jump on to the first, off again, and immediately on to the next. Entirely new to him, they caused Prince Hal a little heartburning; he had never jumped banks of any kind, and I was amused with his performance, for in negotiating them he would take five or six strides along the top, trembling all the way and with his stomach almost touching the bank.

Reading through my diary at the end of the year I was struck by the note I had scribbled concerning another speed event, carried out over an enormous course. The entry ran . . .

"Terrible course. D'Inzeo breaks arm. Garriso damages leg. Navarro breaks neck. Hal goes well. . . ."

Our meeting with General Franco was brief but interesting. I had not expected to shake hands with the only survivor among Europe's three principal Fascist dictators, and I wondered, as we all stood in line, what kind of a personality the Spanish leader would turn out to be. Eventually, the little Caudillo came to me; we shook hands and exchanged a few pleasantries about the horses and the jumping. I cannot therefore truthfully claim to have had much opportunity of observing his character. It seemed to me, however, that in public at any rate the dictator of Spain was just an ordinary mild-mannered man.

But no encounter could match the excitement and fascination of my own first bullfight. Not as a spectator. As a "matador". My practice *corridas* in the safety of the hotel bedroom, a bath towel my "cape" and the bed-post my "bull", turned to reality sooner than I expected.

It happened on the hot, dusty, glorious afternoon of our visit to Monasterio, the estate of the Duques de Pinohermoso who was an old friend of Ruby Holland-Martin's. On a fine ranch not far from El Escorial, the Duke bred some of the fighting bulls of Spain—the *toros bravos* of the arenas. Here, too, were gathered some of the leading matadors, Martorell, Dominguin, Ortega, and others; working with experts of the ranch they were bringing in bulls for careful selection, sorting and testing them for *bravery*—that vital term of assessment in Spain—and deciding which would be sold for meat, which retained for the *corridas*.

I had to conceal a little of my exuberance when the Duke, himself a brilliant horseman, announced:

"And now I will show you the bull ring."

This was his private bull ring, where the day's thrills were to reach their peak within the next hour or two.

Inside, the matadors were making a few practice passes; elementary stuff for these artists, but I marvelled as I watched them play the bulls with perfect control, a lovely style, and an easy, fluent rhythm. Then came a superb display by the Duke, on horseback. All his horses were wonderfully-groomed beauties, but none so magnificent to watch as the classic white thoroughbred he rode into the ring. Carrying in his right hand only a short banderilla, or stick, he played the bulls with tremendous grace, and gave us into the bargain an object lesson in an unusual form of dressage—cantering the horse off any leg, turning in every direction so that the bull's menacing horns, often within an inch of the horse's hide, never quite touched the lovely white coat.

Into the ring, afterwards, was brought a young bull, less "brave" perhaps, but terribly fast and quicker in its turns than the big bulls.

I suspect that the Duke had already sensed my throbbing eagerness to learn by practical experience, for he looked straight into my eyes when he asked, in a clearly challenging tone:

"Would any of our visitors care to try with the cape? To 'have a go'—is that not how you call it?"

The banter in his voice was too much for me. "I would love it," I said boldly, not by any means certain that I spoke the truth.

And down to the ring I jumped, from the high surrounding wall where we had stood watching. I was given a cape and I took a few steps away from the safety of the *barrera*. Suddenly I realized that an interested silence had fallen on the small crowd of Spaniards who stood watching; but an ugly snort from the young bull now facing me shook my brain free of such mild distractions.

I went nearer, and a moment later the bull came at me.

My first pass with the cape was a somewhat graceless twirl that was marred chiefly because I trod on my own toe. Perhaps it was a good thing to have happened; it broke the ice, as it were, and by the time the bull had

141

turned I knew I was no longer frightened, merely exhilarated.

The next flourish with the cape was a good deal more natural and rhythmic, or so it seemed to me, and at the third I found that I could concentrate on the bull following the cape rather than on the movement of the cape in my hands.

"That one was much better, senorita," said a soft, encouraging Spanish voice. I looked up and saw one of the matadors smiling.

"You must fix his attention, always on the cape," he said. "Use the cape wrong, senorita, and the bull he goes for *you* instead."

I tried again, and experienced a millionth part of the glow that must come from a movement of real style when the bull comes charging. By this time I had held out for seven minutes, which was long enough.

An amateur photographer had now come into the ring to take pictures; and unimpressed by the size of my *toro bravo* he had begun joking: "Such a *little* bull. Such a *silly* little bull." He rapidly changed his mind and his colour when the silly little bull took stock of him briefly, charged, found contact, and sent him thumping into the *barrera*. I handed over my cape, wiped my brow, and decided I had done not too badly for a mere English novice—and a woman at that.

I left Madrid with deep regret. There had been no spectacular show jumping victories for me, but the sun, the charm, the Spanish spirit, and the easy-going days had combined to give me, for the first time, I suppose, that sense of living without strain. Before completing the arrangements for shipping Prince Hal back to

England, I gave him a more than usually affectionate farewell, and told him:

"Two years I've been longing for a trip such as this—and now it's you I have to thank for it."

We drove away, out of Spain, into France, through the château country in the valley of the Loire, and north to the Channel, where a gentle drizzle informed us that we were truly nearing home.

Through the summer and on into October Prince Hal added to his already substantial fame. Tosca came into her own as a show jumper of brilliance. Leona went well and won several important competitions. And even the sturdy little Djort, my *petit* Parisian, began the summer season by winning the international trial at Derby and the Ladies' Open Jumping at Richmond. The hectic weeks following our return from Spain culminated in the International Show at the White City during July.

The events had been going for barely an hour when Hal lamed himself on one of the fences. But Leona jumped wonderfully, and together with Marie Delfosse on Fanny Rosa we won the international pair relay race —the only two girls in the event. Leona also achieved second place in the Princess Elizabeth Cup, beaten by Iris Kellett riding Rusty; both horses had jumped clear rounds, but Rusty came through with better timing.

An embarrassment I had not yet dreamed of occurred at the end. The Queen, still then Princess Elizabeth, was presenting the prizes, and I had been too preoccupied or too careless to notice precisely what others were doing about the problem that suddenly hit me: Do you *curtsey* in riding boots? Or just bow? Or what? What had Iris

143

done? I did not know, and I looked down at my grimy breeches; certainly it was too late now to find out. As I walked up the steps and faced the smiling Princess, I decided to bow. But when it came to the point, riding breeches and all, I curtseyed.

One day from the end of the White City Show, Prince Hal recovered from his injury and went magnificently, to win the *Country Life* and Riding Cup; he was also second in the great *Daily Mail* championship, an event I longed to win, and in this there was a minor compensation with the thought that it took Foxhunter to vanquish him—by one-fifth of a second in the final jump-off.

The Harringay Horse of the Year Show brought Tosca and Hal together into glory. Hal carried off the Diana Stakes and Tosca the coveted Lonsdale Memorial Cup. But the surprise of the show was undoubtedly Tosca; a trifle over-ambitious, it seemed, I had entered her for the difficult Prix Caprilli, which involved us in stiff tests of dressage as well as jumping. Much to the astonishment of some of the experts who tended to think that show jumpers knew nothing of dressage, Tosca performed in brilliant style—and won. It was on these performances that she gained me, for the second time, the B.S.J.A. Spurs—a major award of the British Show Jumping Association.

The weeks and the shows flew by, and even while I still revelled in memories of our Spanish tour, the news arrived that we had been selected for Zurich, Geneva, Paris, and Brussels—Tosca's first experience of show jumping abroad.

The tour was a good one for the British team, but

there was no doubt that our Continental rivals were masters of all the show jumping arts. High on our list of memories was the comedy performance of the show jumping year—starring Prince Hal, Nobbler, Colonel Llewellyn and me. It happened during the international relay at Geneva. . . .

As an ex-racehorse perhaps Hal should have gone last, since he is never easy to pull up when he is excited. But in this event he went first, and at the end of our round Harry Llewellyn on Nobbler was to gallop behind us, take from me the traditional relay whip and begin jumping *his* round. It so happened that Hal went round at a fantastic speed, jumping our last fence enormously. Harry came hard on our trail, but not quite fast enough for Prince Hal's tremendous stride; hearing the beating hooves behind him, Hal the racehorse pulled away like a turbo-jet, and Nobbler just managed to catch up as we reached the first fence that Harry was intended to cope with. Unfortunately Harry and I dropped the whip between us as he jumped. So back came the Colonel to retrieve the whip, and I wondered if I should dismount to pick it up in order to save him time. Harry, however, waved me aside with a gallant gesture indicating that it was not a *lady's* task to climb down from her horse; at the same time he began to dismount.

"Began" is the word. He got no further, since with pieces of old string he had tied his stirrups to his spurs after discovering earlier that the stirrups were inclined to become unhitched when jumping Nobbler. Harry Llewellyn was a fixture on his horse.

Frantically he started to untie the strings. By this point the crowd was cheering with delight. Harry solemnly continued, got himself out of the stirrups, picked up the whip and galloped on. If not the most stylish, it was unquestionably the most popular event of the show.

For me, this Continental tour was also marked by a pathetic incident which put a revealing light on the reactions of men and women faced with an emotional disturbance at moments when all emotion should be blending with concentration on the tasks ahead.

In one of the show-jumping cities—it does not matter which—I had a friend who was a first-class horseman, until the night that his young, beautiful, and temperamental fiancée decided to break off their engagement. Next morning I found him hollow-eyed and disconsolate, standing at a street corner gazing at the gutter as if his heart lay shattered in the newly collected heap of litter at his feet. We went to a café opposite, ordered rolls and large cups of coffee, waited until the *garçon* laid them before us.

"You've got to pull yourself together. In two hours you'll be representing your country in a big competition. Can you not try to forget all this till the end of the day?"

The young rider looked at me blankly, then turned his eyes away and murmured, half to himself:

"Can't you see I still love her? That's why I can't stand it. I love her, and I can't. . . ."

And that was more or less all he would say. I tried to make him see sense, but could not shake him out of the lethargy that was now affecting his physical strength as well as his mind.

Later he went into the ring and jumped atrociously. I was convinced that self-pity had lost him that competition. And my thoughts went back to the night, only a few weeks earlier, during Harringay's Horse of the Year Show. I knew what it felt like and the same sort of thing had nearly knocked me off my balance. Was it merely chance, I wondered, or was it some fundamental difference in the mental workings of women and men which determined whether you went to pieces?

I am going to tell this story because it does show that it is not always easy to reconcile show jumping and some of the things one most values in life. But it is not the sort of story one particularly enjoys telling.

For some time I had known someone whom I not only liked very much but who had come to mean more to me than anyone else. I was and still am quite sure that one should not be in a hurry over marriage—it is worth too much. But I was beginning seriously to think and feel that I was ready to consider it. One thing, however, was plain. I would need to be ready whole-heartedly to abandon show jumping if necessary, and I could not honestly say I was as sure about things as that. I thought he understood this—so it came as a shock when he met me at the close of the first day at Harringay and said:

"I suppose it is vital for you to go on this jaunt to Paris and Geneva. Or is it?"

"What on earth do you mean?" I asked.

"Oh nothing. It's just that I see no reason for waiting much longer before we marry—and I think it's time you began making up your mind about whether it's me or Hal and Tosca you're in love with."

I must have looked rather upset for he added:

"Don't leap to conclusions. I'm not asking you to give

147

up show jumping, merely to think again about this trip to Europe next month. After all, there'll be other opportunities to go abroad."

Before I could comment he went on: "It so happens that I take the whole month off from business. Surely it is worth swopping one tour for our honeymoon. Or don't you think that's important enough?"

Now it was not the first time—nor perhaps will it be the last—that my friends had remarked, "Pat's just a horsy girl, no time for men . . . I play second fiddle to Tosca, of course". . . . I take it in good heart, but never before had it come home quite so forcibly that men might be jealous of my work.

The next forty-eight hours were like a nightmare. Prince Hal was playing up as never before and his temperament had to be nursed with care. The Prix Caprilli and the Lonsdale Memorial Stakes loomed ahead. I had to meet people and to keep up appearances in various official engagements, but they seemed quite unreal. I felt utterly unnerved and unable to concentrate. I did not sleep that night.

Next morning I looked round the Harringay course and scrutinized the teams. They were mostly men. At that moment there came a sudden glow of determination that no man should beat me that day.

Tosca, the grey mare, was magnificent. We pulled off the Lonsdale Cup, the Prix Caprilli, and the B.S.J.A. Spurs.

CHAPTER 9

ALONE AT MISERDEN

THE Monday morning was bright and icy—January the fourteenth, 1952, with my brother Ronald home from the theological college at Ely where he was nearing the end of his training for the church, a sphere of work on which his mind was now firmly set.

Mother and I had sat up till the early hours, intermittently gossiping, planning, writing letters, and making up the guest-house accounts. She had made a happy world of the guest house at Miserden, and at least during spring and summer the place had become something of a rural united nations centre, for we had visitors from a score of countries; some came to ride, some to tramp the Cotswold hills and valleys, some merely to lounge and recuperate from the nervy turmoil of city life. Mother and I had been greatly perturbed at the start of the year when our friend Ruby Holland-Martin, a brilliant member of the British show jumping team, had suffered an appalling injury while hunting. He now lay in an Oxford hospital with a broken neck—a disaster that was to end his career as an active horseman.

The winter had been slack, but there had been a number of Christmas visitors, and now, in January, we had several students as guests; a trio of newcomers from New Zealand were also due the following week. Quite suddenly Mother had become set on having a small party of neighbours on the Sunday evening. George Arthurs, the Miserden Park Agent, who with his wife had helped so immensely when we had first come to Miserden and whose sympathy and practical assistance were always ready at hand, Tony and Marjorie Frenkel from Waverley Farm, firm friends and parents of my god-daughter, were there, and so was Mr. Thorpe, the Rector, whose tact and consideration I was soon to value so much. We had some music provided by George, Mother and Ronald, and altogether it was a cheerful party just like old times at Beaufort. Perhaps particularly cheered for us by the thought that after a long period in debt we were beginning to make good financially. The day had really been a family one for we had been together all through it and had begun by making our communions together at the charming little village church.

I was not up the following morning when Mother rose early to take two Chinese boys to Stroud station—they had become almost members of the family as they always spent their school holidays with us. Ronald was going up to London that morning on his motor-bike (which Mother and I both considered a horribly dangerous machine), so it was he who took Mother some tea, saw them to the car, rushed back to get the railway tickets, and finally waved good-bye as the jeep swung into the lane and climbed up past the village tree.

It was Ronald too who, wondering why Mother was so long—he had promised to say good-bye before going to London—met George Arthurs and learnt that Mother was dead. By the War Memorial on the Stroud road the car had skidded on a sheet of ice, there was no rail to stop it and it fell over the steep bank into the hollow below. The students were safe but Mother had been killed at once. It was Ronald who told me.

I do not know what would have happened had we not had so much to do. There was no time to let the awful paralysing feeling of grief get a hold when I had to cater for guests (our cook had recently gone), to see to the horses, to try to face the facts of the situation, and to master the books and the prospects. But we both had an incredibly strong feeling that Mother was with us— her happiness still pervaded the house—and that helped more than anything. Then again the wretched formalities were redeemed so completely for us by the wonderfully sincere affection and thoughtfulness of friends, especially those at Miserden. But in a sense also there was never any doubt about what we ought to do.

Ronald and I had soon decided that, with Wing Commander and Mrs. Sinclair's permission, we would try to carry on at Miserden House. There was no need to worry about the house—the Sinclairs were all generosity. But clearly we should need a housekeeper now, since I would be away so often, and perhaps we ought to have something in hand for there would be death duties as well as additional expenses. In these problems we found a new friend (more than a legal adviser to us now), Mr. Eric Watterson, but alas, lost an old one. Poor Leona had to go. She was a valuable mare, and since I would never have parted with either Tosca or Hal, it had to be her; a good offer had already come from Switzerland, and after engaging a housekeeper for Miserden I made arrangements for taking her across, together with a young pony also to be bought by Leona's new owner.

Early in March I took Leona and the pony to Folkestone, slept on the train with them that night, and boarded the Channel boat next morning. The only other passenger was a man who was taking a string of brood mares to France.

The Channel was rough and the Captain hummed and hawed about whether he would allow us to sail; he obviously regretted his decision when we hit the storm soon after leaving harbour. The crossing was terrible, with sea water pouring across the decks and into the sheltered holds where Leona, the pony, and the mares were standing. The horses were soon soaked and at one stage we grew nervous for their safety, for the rolling ship tossed about the valuable mares, some of them heavy in foal; they slithered pitifully around the wet plank flooring and there was little we could do to soothe them. Eventually we reached Boulogne, where I put my two horses into the goods train that would take us non-stop across France. The goods van was old, and could have been scrawled with the words of that classic inscription from the First World War: 40 Men, or 8 Horses. Before the train pulled out I had fifteen minutes to make a dash for the nearest *épicerie* where I bought a bottle of red wine and a large cheese; it was now dark, and I could not find a place to buy bread.

We started the long, slow jolting journey. I had laid straw everywhere in the van, opened the sliding door, roped it off to stop it moving—for this was our sole means of light and air—pushed a bale of straw across the opening to allay the more intolerable draughts, and settled Leona at one end, the young pony at the other. I bedded down on straw in the middle . . . to improve my French by torchlight (with a book!).

There was snow on the ground in France, but I had brought with me a warm sleeping bag which, together with the wine and cheese, kept me reasonably comfortable. The worst part was the noise; we stopped in sidings, miles out of any town, where the shunting and the rattling of the truck drove all three of us to distraction. Through the night the train would suddenly jerk to a standstill, throwing Leona or the pony perilously near to the open door. After one such incident I clambered down to the track, raced the length of the train, stumbling in the darkness, and had a tactful conversation, in French, with the engine driver and his mate. We were carrying a pair of valuable horses, I told them, and would they please try to shunt a little more carefully. The engine driver gave me a graceful bow, took my hand to assist me down from the footplate with the air of a man about to take the floor for a waltz, and gave me a gallant if satirical assurance that from now on he would shunt like a ballerina. I laughed to myself as I walked back to rejoin the horses; but he kept his word, and the next lot of shunting was smoother.

The wine soon gave out and I went on to cheese and water; even this became a problem, for as often as not I had to walk several hundred yards to find a tap where I could fill two buckets for the horses, and twice during the first night the train began moving off just as I was placing the buckets on the floor of our truck. I ran alongside, grimly holding a rail to hoist myself inside, while the tottering buckets slopped half their precious contents over the floor.

Aside from these alarms, however, it was an oddly peaceful journey, despite the noise; the horses were good companions, and there was time for thought and reverie such as I had not known since childhood. In the early hours of the second morning we rattled into Basle, where I saw the horses safely into a clean, comfortable Swiss electric train, met the new owner who took me by car to his lakeside home at Biel, where I gave my grimy limbs a good bath, and sat down to a vast midday meal. The next day I showed them how to handle Leona and the pony, who seemed none the worse for their gruelling trip, then went to Wengen where I was to spend four sunny days with Mimi, the sister of my old friend Sam Koechlin.

Mimi and her husband—the Swiss show jumper Mario Mylius—were staying with their two children in the delightful Wengen chalet they shared with another family, and here I helped with the cooking in the intervals between long, energetic skiing excursions. A week later, after a brief pause in Paris where I bought some inexpensive clothes, I was back home at Miserden, a little wealthier after the sale of Leona, a little more fortified for the task of preparing Hal and Tosca for the show jumping season.

The importance to me of a certain young woman, a slim, determined-looking girl called Pauline Sykes, had never been clearer than during the weeks that followed. Pauline, known as "Paul" to Miserden in particular and to most of the show jumping world, had joined me as a working assistant in the winter of 1949 when she was

154

eighteen. The daughter of parents who owned a confectionery shop in Bedford, she had a natural love of and a supernatural genius with horses, blended these with a physical strength which seemed impossible for her build, and within a few years had become indispensable to my busy routine. She became my companion around the shows, abroad as well as in Britain, and devoted herself to the horses—Prince Hal, above all—with a degree of efficiency and singlemindedness so high that I realized few show jumpers anywhere could count themselves as fortunate in their choice of employees. During this summer of 1952 Paul threw herself into the work with an energy even greater than usual.

For at least two months Prince Hal was a problem. I had allowed him to be sent for training purposes to the Olympic Games quarters, where he, with his thoroughbred temperament, had not appreciated the rigours of army discipline. Perhaps he missed his girls at home; but whatever the reason he returned after three weeks having lost weight and confidence. Tosca, however, opened her season with a bang, went from strength to strength, victory to victory, and seemed well-nigh unbeatable.

In June we went to the Richmond Royal Horse Show. Tosca began by tying for the first place in the Jubilee Challenge Cup, then, as if mildly irritated by this unsatisfactory result, went on magnificently to win both the Albert Duke of York trophy and the Coronation Championship. When we arrived home that night a letter from Switzerland informed us that Leona had already started winning at Continental shows, and my conscience about parting with her was eased. Then, hard on the heels of this cheering news came a second letter announcing that another horse had kicked Leona and broken her leg—a tragedy indeed for the gay, cheeky little mare.

From now until the end of August our programme was tightly packed, for one result of the impact of Mother's death was that I took on a volume of work and competitions demanding every ounce of concentration.

First I gave Tosca a bracing week at Brighton, where she carried off the South of England Championship, then took her, together with Prince Hal, to a Midlands show; between them they shared first place in the Midlands Championship. Early in July came the Royal Show at Newton Abbot, where Queen Elizabeth was among the visitors; and that day, for the third time, I won the Walwyn Challenge Cup, on Tosca—in 1949 it had been won by Leona, the year before that by Finality. For the Athlone Cup, Hal and Tosca went superbly—and tied again.

By the end of August Hal was well into his stride, had won the B.S.J.A. Ladies' Championship at Blackpool, the Ladies' Championship at Royal Windsor, and the Grand Prix at Cardiff. But it was Tosca's summer. At the White City International Horse Show she played a major role in the team that brought us the Nations' Cup, and became equal first prizewinner of the Selby Cup. In the *Daily Mail* championship it was my friend Brian Butler on Tankard. Drat that man and his horse! Tosca had jumped brilliantly in this event (where I had been runner-up the previous year), and was beaten by Tankard for the sum of four-fifths of a second.

In October, at Harringay's Horse of the Year Show, Tosca's astonishing march of success became ever faster and more melodious. The Diana Stakes, the Lonsdale Memorial Cup (for the second year running), and the B.S.J.A. Spurs (the second time for Tosca). I began to feel that for £150 she had been quite a good "buy," and told her so.

At Harringay, too, I had an amusing experience with young dirt track riders, whose organization had invited me to be guest of honour at a dinner, then to present prizes to winners of their championship races. After a very fine dinner I was ushered towards the red carpet, conducted to the edge of the track, and entertained to a spectacle of daredevil riding by young heroes of the speedway. It was highly impressive, for the lightweight motor cycles were stripped to the bone, without brakes, and sent hurtling round the corners at breathtaking speed while the riders nonchalantly trailed a steel-capped boot to steady themselves.

Eventually, the races ended and the chief victor named, I was asked to make a short speech before presenting the award—a silver cup and a handsome cheque. The young man, bashful in the limelight, came forward to wait while I unburdened myself. I referred briefly to my pleasure in the evening's exploits, spoke of how well the young man had won his way to the front after the major initiative had been held by another rider during the whole of the race, until our young hero popped through, and then—speaking directly to the champion, expecting an appropriate comment—I said:

"I thought it was a wonderful race . . . congratulations."

Looking as benevolent as I felt after the evening's

entertainment, I paused. The young man reddened, licked his lips, and forced out a reply.

"Were it?" he said. And that was all.

I hurriedly handed over his cheque and trophy, feeling that further words of mine could be only anti-climax.

After Harringay, Paris, where I took Tosca and Hal, and where, oddly enough, it became Prince Hal's turn to sail smoothly through the show to win the most notable events so far in his brief career at international competitions. Hal not only won, with a superb display, the important Prix du Champion, but went so well that before leaving Paris he had collected also the title of Leading Horse of the Show. And this great effort, coupled with Tosca's consistently good performances, gave me the official distinction of becoming the leading rider as well as the leading woman rider. We travelled on to Brussels where, on the last day, Hal and Tosca between them jumped to a triumphant conclusion for their first joint effort abroad—and won me the Grand Prix. The gruelling test for this event was largely a question of speed where the rider, employing two horses, must carry out a breakneck quick-change from one mount to the other in order to save seconds. Tosca and Prince Hal responded to each other like a pair of young sweethearts, keeping close together and allowing me to jump from one saddle to the other in minimum time. I returned to England for an enjoyable spell of hunting with the Cotswold hounds, and life, busy as ever though a shade less hectic, began once more to be worth living.

What a wonderful year it had been and how I wished that Mother could have been with me to share it! Without Mother's plans and efforts and sacrifices there would have been no *annus mirabilis,* and without her presence it was not the same thing. How she would have loved to see the grey mare who had once had trouble with her gates and fences become Great Britain's leading horse of the year, a truly amazing achievement in her first full season as a front-rank show jumper in open contest with some of the best horses the world had to offer.

To cap it all, Prince Hal was placed third among the nation's horses.

I went back for ten days to my friends at Wengen, in Switzerland, to the winter sun and the fresh snows, to that whole exhilaration of individual effort on skis—and wished that *my* skis might contrive enough of a partnership with my legs and arms to achieve, if not the glow that Tosca and Hal brought me, then at least an occasional clear round on the white slopes of Scheidegg and the Lauberhorn.

CHAPTER 10

"WHAT A HORSE!"

MOST yellow objects in the lush mansion called
Lavaronde were gold. Luncheon began at twelve-thirty
and ended around five. The *pâté de foie gras* alone must
have been worth the weekly wages of two skilled Englishmen or twelve Algerians. Musing on the bread and apple
snacks I tended to give myself at Miserden, it was, I
thought, quite a day.

This visit to Algiers had come in a somewhat round-
about fashion. Harry Llewellyn and his wife were
travelling to Australia to do some judging at the Sydney
Horse Show; on the way back, said Harry, he wanted to
jump in the international events at Rome early in May,
and we worked out a programme whereby I would take
two of his horses—Monty, and a novice called St. Teilo—
first to Algiers, then to Marseilles, on to Nice, thence
to Rome. There were show jumping contests in each
place, and I would have with me my own Tosca and
Prince Hal. Colonel Nicoll would ride Harry's horses
at Nice, and Harry would take over when he, and they,
arrived in Rome. Our British team-mate Geoffrey
Gibbon was also coming along, and it was with Geoffrey
that I drove across France at the end of March on the
first leg of our rather complex Cook's tour of the
Continental shows.

Clearing the second fence with Prince Hal during the International
Horse Show Ladies' Débutante Competition

try a new sport. Driving Authentic in the Amateur Class at the
White City

Tosca and Prince Hal add their own greetings as I stop to pet
dogs Bliss and Windy before setting out for our daily exerc

Chiefly to prove how truly British, hardy, and outdoor-girlish I could be if I tried hard, I bathed in the cold sea at La Ciotat before crossing the Mediterranean—in a plane carrying a hundred passengers—to Algiers. On arrival, we and other competitors were met almost literally with fanfares, and after a friendly if heady cocktail reception, at which we were welcomed by M. André Mathiot, the show's president, we were consigned to our hotel in the centre of Algiers. There followed a noisy, restless night throughout which three-quarters of the Arab and other native populations of North Africa seemed to congregate screaming below *my* bedroom window. Interesting, nevertheless.

On Good Friday morning we were collected by André Mathiot for a drive to his estate a hundred miles out of Algiers. He began talking rapid French to us at 8.30 in the morning, and did not pause for breath (or so it seemed) until we got back at night some fourteen hours later.

"Come to lunch at Lavaronde," he had said, among other things—and "lunch" was a curious understatement for the banquet to come.

The estate called Lavaronde was by Cleopatra out of the Arabian Nights, with a flavour from Marie Antoinette thrown in. A technicolor palace across the mountains, through the native villages and beyond the citrus groves, Monsieur Mathiot kept "a few horses". . . his matter-of-factness was beginning to delight me . . . and I observed that he also kept a few stables; these were backyard palaces, so to speak, where equipment was mostly in triplicate, where the horses' nameplates on the doors were all but jewelled, and where in general I felt that I ought to remove my dusty shoes. Monsieur Mathiot also kept a private arena, which turned out to be a kind of oriental White City, though richer in facilities and without trolley buses passing its gates. The arena was no less than a fully-furnished show ring, with grounds perfectly tended, with permanent banks, with innumerable fences, with its own water jump, and with a high raised platform for the "judges." Whether a single day's "judging" had ever been performed in the place, or a show ever held, I did not discover. But its munificence was certainly impressive. Not far away was the Mathiot coach house—a strange touch, this, on the fringe of the African desert—with old and "original" coaches brought from England, glittering harnesses, decorated saddles and riding whips, the whole scene looking like a mirage of some corner of the Buckingham Palace Mews. As for the home farm, I found its most striking appeal in the workshop; here were row upon row of well-kept tools of the highest quality; you selected your hammer from a rack containing a hundred, your screwdriver from among the serried ranks of a thousand or thereabouts. Lavaronde, in short, had pretty well everything.

In the house itself, all was silver, or gold, or velvet, or tapestried, or Napoleonic, or in some way precious. André's middle name happened to *be* Napoleon, and about Napoleon furniture and décor he was most enthusiastic; the rooms and halls reflected this passion. Yet for a good deal of the year, I gathered, he lived in Algiers; perhaps, after all, Lavaronde was his little place in the country.

About the luncheon. *The Luncheon.* And I mean the five-hour luncheon.

At about twelve-thirty we were ushered out of doors to a cool place beneath tall palms, where orange trees flanked a long table. Gleaming on the white cloths was an array of silver and fine glass.

Having finished a tour of the entire estate, we were delighted when André said: "You would like a cocktail?"

Expecting the usual aperitif I said I would like a cocktail, and having finished it I said at once that I would like another, for these were champagne cock-tails of a delicacy I had never encountered . . . mixed with orange juice from the fruit of the trees nearby.

Then we sat down to lunch, the party including Georges Calmon, who was jumping at the Show, Jean Bridel, Monsieur and Madame Roblin, Geoffrey Gibbon, and me—with Monsieur Mathiot presiding like a Grand Seigneur of some more gracious era. I cannot now remember the full list of culinary glories laid before us by two Algerian servants, but they included *crevettes, pâté de foie gras, saumon fumé, asperges,* breasts of fowl in wine, caviar, cheeses galore, and a variety of fruits. Eight courses, each with the appropriate wine; the champagne had been shipped from Rheims, the hock from Germany, the Chablis from France, the liqueurs from all over. There was, as it happened, no hint of local patriotism: the only wine that seemed to be missing was Algerian.

Eventually we reached the last and longest course of all, the brandy, the coffee, and the cigars. At first I was a little resistant to the "dares" of my male companions, but finally, on the principle of "try anything once" I gave in, and smoked my cigar to the bitter, the decidedly bitter, end.

We rose from the table a few minutes before half-past five and drove back to Algiers. Monsieur Mathiot's little luncheon made all thoughts of supper a gross vulgarity.

Altogether, the visit was memorable for its leisure pursuits rather than show jumping successes. I was not meeting Hal and Tosca until I went on to Marseilles, and at Algiers I had a bad fall, cutting my face while schooling Harry's horse Monty in an effort to gain his confidence. Monty, too, was shaken by the fall, but rallied so brilliantly in the competition that on the last day he almost won the Grand Prix, which would have brought £200 and a set of gold buttons; as things turned out we had to be content with third place. We also went bathing in the sea that day (less than fifty miles away it could have been skiing), and on the beach devised a ridiculous but entertaining pastime· a race meeting for the enormous though harmless beetles which abounded. We constructed a beach arena, built miniature jumps and ditches, and cheered on our respective beetles to the final winning post. Back at the hotel that night, I discovered one crawling in my small canvas bag and decided it was high time I packed for Marseilles.

Waiting there, in the devoted charge of my assistant Pauline, were Tosca and Prince Hal, the latter somewhat crazy after a long spell without work. Next morning, I schooled both horses in the show ring and was amused to overhear a number of derisive comments as officials, competitors, and privileged visitors watched Hal's excited antics.

164

"What a horse to bring to an international show," snapped one man.

This left me untroubled; but I liked to think that Hal turned his gaze for the sole purpose of sizing-up this complacent creature on the sidelines, who stood pointing his finger or nodding his small head at all and sundry with the air of the man who seemed to know what was what in the realms of horseflesh.

In the show that night, after jumping an awkward first round where he twisted and fought, Prince Hal settled down like a lamb, went like a stag, and jumped three astonishing rounds to win the "doubles and trebles" competitions—fences in pairs and threes. Then he carried on faultlessly throughout the Show, jumping eleven rounds without touching a fence.

As the critic had sourly said: "What a horse to bring to an international show!"

During the gap between shows from Marseilles to Nice I went to Arles, the Provençal setting for Van Gogh's turbulent life and art, and also the home of my friend the Comte de Roux, whose daughter had stayed with us at Miserden. He took me on a brief, fascinating tour of the Camargue, where the salt marshes look like natural film sets, and where men raise little fighting bulls. And over by the sea at Stes. Maries de Mer we ended with a picnic in the Comte's *cabane* on the deserted beach, a simple turf hut, windowless, with a hole in the roof to carry away the smoke from your wood fire on the floor.

At Nice I met the horses again, along with two more of our British team, Bill Hanson and Wilfred White; at once we joined the teams of our rival countries for an inspection of the course, where the entire show jumping community began pulling long faces. The cause was a trick bank, nearly eight feet high, narrow, perilous, and coming to a point at the top. It had been constructed the night before with wet sods, had baked in the morning sun, and would obviously give no grip for any horse.

An unfair fence. The outcry grew. Complaints from all quarters rumbled through to the show committee, but the committee decided against us, declared the fence to be a right and proper work, and announced that having built the thing, it had to be jumped.

The competition began, and the first man in was Carlos Figueroa, who had won the King George V Cup in Britain. His horse reached the mountainous trick bank, and fell. The next rider jumped it badly and nearly fell. So did the next. Towards the end I came in with Tosca, who jumped a brilliant fast round, then faced the bank.

Tosca jumped so big that she almost cleared the whole business; but across the lip of the bank she just touched on the far side, turned half circle in the air and landed on her back with her feet against the bank. I was pinned underneath her.

She rolled over and scrambled upright; unfortunately she could not help but do this at my expense, trampled me in several places, and ground me into the sand. Suddenly there came a biting pain; as the mare struggled to stand upright, one of her studs jabbed hard into the flesh of my leg while I lay half buried, spluttering the sand and grit out of my mouth and eyes. By the time Tosca was free and her weight removed, the numbness in my leg was such that I barely realized I was injured. So I pulled myself up, climbed aboard and jumped two more fences, wondering why the groups of nearby people were shouting at me to stop. Then I was carted off to hospital.

The surgery involved removing pieces of muscle from my leg, which meant that I was out for the rest of the show. Unhappily, the surgery performed on Prince Hal by a French blacksmith was less skilled, for in changing his shoes the blacksmith damaged Hal's pedal bone so badly that the horse was out of action for nearly three months afterwards. When, days later, we reached Rome, a doctor who renewed the dressing on my leg baldly announced that he hoped it was not turning gangrenous, and to be on the safe side packed me off again to hospital.

Physically better but in a thoroughly bad temper I came out of hospital on the first day of the Rome Show. I was lame. Hal was lame. Tosca was lame. A bright prospect for jumping.

Tosca and I, however, were still in sufficiently sound wind and limb to have a go, so into the ring we went. The poor horse had rather lost her nerve, which was hardly surprising, and since I had no longer the leg power to kick her into the fences, which was what she needed, it was also unsurprising that she stumbled in the middle of a triple fence. Tosca half fell and sent me swinging around her neck. She straddled the next fence, a triple bar across water, yet still bravely plunged on, with me unseated. Somehow, I recovered my balance, returned to the saddle and finished the round. But at the end of the day, Tosca and I were lamer than ever,

167

she hopping on her near hind leg, I on my right.

The compensating triumph of the Rome Show was Bill Hanson on Monarch, winning the Grand Prix. Bill received as his prize a handsome Vespa motor cycle, and delighted the crowd by riding it noisily around the ring in place of the traditional dignified canter on the winning horse.

Into Vatican City went the international show jumping teams, Italian, French, British, Austrian, and German, before we left Rome. A meeting with the Pope had been arranged.

Through the decorated corridors and ante-rooms, past the vividly-uniformed Vatican Guards, we walked slowly to the audience chamber, a little nervous at the prospect of coming face to face with Pius XII, for what possible harmony could the Pontiff strike with a motley crowd of "horsey" athletes?

The Pope settled our shynesses from the start. With great charm and abundant conversation he talked to each man and woman as if horsemanship were among his major enthusiasms—and talked, moreover, invariably in the language of the visitor concerned; his English, especially, was strikingly competent.

Suddenly, as I watched the demeanour of the others, I flushed with lonely embarrassment. My right leg was stiff as a board, and I realized it would be quite impossible to kneel in front of the Pope when it came to my turn. The question was: should I bow, and say nothing, or should I make a painful effort and risk stumbling, or should I perhaps explain to the Pope that I had injured my leg and was unable to bend it? The last solution seemed the best, yet how on earth could I straightaway launch into meaningless complex apologies about an injury?

Nevertheless, I had to do something, and when the moment arrived I began mumbling my explanation as I took hold of the Pope's outstretched hand. He at once cut short the apology with a smile and a brief gesture showing that he fully understood my predicament, and went on to ask:

"How is your beloved country?"

The Pope also spoke of Sir Winston Churchill, hoping that the Premier was in good health and spirits, and concluded with some questions on the horses and the week's events. Our audience at the Vatican was the climax of a tour which had been packed with interest and incident.

Home to England far too quickly, by way of the loveliest of all Italian cities, Siena and Florence. And so back to earth for a summer of English show jumping.

A summer, I might add, which Tosca and Prince Hal, once they were recovered from their ailments, turned into the most exhilarating jumping season of my life. All my springtime gallivanting in Africa and Europe had run away with more money than I cared to afford; it was vital, therefore, that Hal and Tosca paid their way.

This they did. The two horses could hardly have done better if they had been able to put their heads together in a conscious, prizewinning effort to plan my budget. In mid-June I took Tosca to the Richmond Horse Show; she came out of it with the Jubilee Cup, the Sir Archibald Weigall Memorial Gold Cup, the Albert Duke of York trophy and the Coronation

Championship. Next stop Brighton, where Tosca had her usual celebration by the sea. In fact, she won every day.

By the end of the week Tosca had completed a period of jumping, including important puissances or test competitions, together with international championships, in which she negotiated more than two hundred fences without touching. It was a stupendous achievement. Then at the White City International Show the following month, Prince Hal joined Tosca for another spate of victories.

Our English summer, during which for many weeks I had taken Tosca and Hal to an average of four shows a week, turned to autumn—and Harringay. In autumn, as some wag once said, a young show jumper's fancy heavily turns to thoughts of the Harringay Spurs and the Victor Ludorum Championship. So it must have been with Tosca. She won them, and again became the leading Show Jumper in Great Britain.

After Harringay—Harrisburg, New York, Toronto, and points west. Far, far west.

Our trip to the United States, in the autumn of 1953, was due largely to Colonel Harry Llewellyn's ineffable push and go. For a long time we had wanted to compete at the international shows in America and Canada, but for a long time, too, it seemed we might be hamstrung for lack of cash . . . until Harry got into his stride. Eventually, our friend Colonel Mike Ansell, chairman of the British Show Jumping Association, fixed up an official British team, and after hectic preparations at Miserden to ensure a more or less smooth passage while I was absent, I sallied forth to the farewell party in London which went on all night—except for eight minutes while I dozed off.

The team consisted of Colonel Llewellyn, Bill Hanson, and me. Our horses were Foxhunter and Lady Jane, Tosca and Prince Hal, Talisman and The Monarch. Harry and I agreed to take the last-named pair across the Atlantic for Bill, who was already in New York. My friend Pauline was coming as usual.

Some people can cross the Atlantic without trouble. With others trouble seems to follow them. It certainly followed us, from the moment we crossed the tarmac at London Airport. First it was Tosca, who had never been at peace in traffic, breaking out into a cold drip sweat at the roar of aircraft engines. Then it was Foxhunter, who became startled when a jet screamed over. We trundled the horseboxes out to the runway before unloading, then put Monarch into the plane, followed by Talisman, Tosca, and Prince Hal.

Not until we came to Foxhunter did we discover that the doorway to our plane was sixteen hands high. Foxhunter is seventeen. So we stripped the coverings from his back, warned him to bend his knees going in, and sighed with relief when he did so. But as luck would have it, an aircraft engine suddenly started up behind us, Foxhunter looked back, hit his head against the doorway, and almost brained himself.

In time, however, everyone appeared to be neat and comfortable, and as the plane began its long taxi before the take-off, I settled back and said to Pauline:

"Bill Hanson said to be careful about The Monarch—he's a bad traveller."

The words acted like a witch's curse. As we gathered

speed, The Monarch started panicking. He threw himself around, struggling violently inside his crate, and a moment later was down on his belly. Then, horror-stricken, we saw him kicking at the sides of the crate. A splintering of wood followed, and out of the gaps came his hind legs, waving within an inch of Prince Hal's head.

"Warn the pilot! And pass me the morphia!" I cried.

CHAPTER 11

SHOW JUMPING IN AMERICA
AND CANADA

THEY did not enlighten me, alas, about the possible effects of morphia upon the central nervous system—of horses as well as human beings. I could hardly know, therefore, that the immediate result of a morphia injection might be wildly stimulating. Hoping for the best, I took up the hypodermic and banged the stuff into The Monarch as our plane taxied across the air strip.

We pleaded with the pilot not to get us airborne until the horses were calmer; and it was just as well that the trouble reached its peak when it did, for if we had ever left the ground, the careers of crew, passengers, and half a dozen sad-looking show jumping horses would doubtless have come to a sudden end. The Monarch kicked yet more wildly, and within a few seconds it was obvious that he would soon be out of his crate.

"O.K. Next stop London Airport," called out one of the crew. And back we came nearly a mile across the runway to the ramp from where we started. But the ramp was gone, and so were the ground staff. We tumbled out of the aircraft and prepared to unload the horses. A little man in uniform and peaked cap walked from the shadows to say:

"I thought you'd be in Shannon by now." I gave him

a sour glance, hitched up my skirt and got back to work.

Since The Monarch had entered the aircraft first, he could only be extricated last, a process which took up considerable time. He was by this point not the most popular horse in the team and was firmly informed that he was being sent to Coventry (in fact he was flown over next day in a crate large enough for an elephant).

After readjusting all the fittings in the rear of the plane, installing the five better-behaved horses and settling ourselves comfortably we took off without incident. Pilot and crew were considerate and very friendly, invited me into the cockpit and showed me the works.

Coming in over Shannon, flying low across the Limerick country, I realized this was my first sight of Ireland since my eventful visit in 1948, and I pointed excitedly down towards Adare, saying to the pilot, a young American:

"Look! That's where I used to go hunting—a wonderful country for riding."

"What kind of hunting did you do?" he asked.

"Fox hunting, of course," I said.

The urban-minded flyer paused for a moment, before spilling out a question fit to turn the English sportsman whitehaired.

"Say, what calibre rifle do you folks use for fox hunting?"

Rifle! Heaven preserve us! I thought of the Master of the Limerick, pictured the meet with hounds and riders setting off in the crispy brightness of an autumn morning, looked sharply at this technician of the twentieth century, and replied, with what I hoped was kindly tolerance:

"We don't use rifles—you see, hunting is an old English sport. We hunt the fox with hounds while we follow on horses." Then I quickly changed the subject.

We landed at Shannon, had dinner, refuelled, took off once more and headed for the Atlantic. The horses travelled like old hands. Prince Hal was especially virtuous, though this was because he passed the entire flight eating; altogether he munched his way through eight hay nets. Early next morning we touched down at Gander, Newfoundland, refuelled again and reached New York about eight o'clock. Hal was not the only gourmand, for by nine o'clock I was attacking my third breakfast; we were, after all, five hours behind London time, had consumed one breakfast on the plane, another at Gander—and it seemed unfriendly to ignore the fruit juice, coffee, and thickly-buttered rolls placed before me on my first morning in the United States.

After coping with the photographers we loaded the horses into imposing trucks bound for the first international show, at Harrisburg—a city halfway between Philadelphia and Pittsburgh, surrounded by townships of Pennsylvania taking their names from the map of England: York, Carlisle, Reading, Lancaster. Then we went into New York to bathe, change, take a little "snort" — that vastly overworked Americanism for "drink"—and saunter around the great city gaping at the skyscrapers, Wall Street, enormous new cars, Broadway, and the bustle which spells America. Uncounted millions of tourists had done it all before me, but no description ever lives up to the first personal experience of the place.

When we heard that the horses had arrived safely in Harrisburg next day we boarded a night plane for Cincinnati—our second airborne night—and from there travelled on to Louisville, Kentucky, for a brief visit to the lovely estate of Oxmore, run by the hospitable Tommy Bullett, an old friend of Harry Llewellyn's. Then followed, in the space of two days before the show jumping began, the kind of rapid tour which Americans can contemplate without a qualm. Oxmore's stables I found fascinating, with their un-English architecture, their slatted floors with modern drainage, their comfortable boxes for the horses, and their ingenious sun trap windows. I was also taken out to the "Blue Grass" country around Lexington, the centre of thoroughbred raising—but the blue grass at this time was a sadly burned brown, following a drought which had made farmers desperate. I saw some of the celebrated studs, with horses like Nasrullah, Blenheim, and Mahmoud, and at the fabulous Calumet Stud, a holy of holies among such places, was impressed by Citation, the leading horse in America, and his sire Bull Lee.

Wherever we journeyed, someone would cry out from time to time:

"Hey, we're comin' to a dry county—better have a quick snort before we get to the border, huh?"

And so, four or five times, we paused for a quick snort before we got to a border. At one country saloon we watched the Turpin-Olsen fight on television, and were saddened by Turpin's spiritless display. Another jaunt took us to the famous Churchill Downs, scene of the

At London Airport with Foxhunter and Col. Llewellyn at the start of our trip to the United States in 1953

(*Below*) On the King Ranch in Texas I take a turn with the lead ox while helping with the round-up

Tosca views with astonishment our transformation into cowgirl and cowpony

Tosca, Windy, the bantams and myself in the yard at Miserden

(*Below*) I part company with Tosca at the Dublin Spring Show, 1954, after a great build-up for positively our first appearance

Tosca during her clear round in the final of the Queen Elizabeth II
Cup at the White City, July 1954

Kentucky Derby. My impression, seeing horses at work, was that the going seemed dead—with sand and dirt suggesting none of the "spring" provided by the turf of an English racecourse.

That day, before the return to Harrisburg, we went boating on the Ohio river, landed our well-equipped launch on the Indiana side of the water so that I could climb out to pick some "Indiana grairss", and returned to Oxmore in the setting October sun to finish the tour with a rousing party and a final round of "snorts".

Prince Hal jumped superbly in the Harrisburg show, won the individual championship and four other events, and was unbeaten; by the end of the show the British team were victorious in seven out of the eleven events. But Tosca, unhappily, damaged a leg in the same spot as at Rome, and thereby damaged her morale for the rest of the tour.

The morning of our arrival from Harrisburg into New York, for the second of the international competitions, included a roaring reception which had everything except the ticker-tape shower which is traditionally reserved for national heroes, fourth-term presidents and victorious generals. Aside from the Americans, the show jumping teams were drawn from Great Britain, Canada, and Ireland—not a huge contingent; and we were ushered into the largest bus I have ever seen to be transported, we were told, to a meeting with the Mayor of New York. For a moment I was a little bored at the prospect. Then the bus started.

We were given a police escort, a motorized squadron of tough, screen-like cops who seemed intent on proving to us that their sirens worked precisely as depicted by

Hollywood. Their wailing scream cleared everything off the New York streets, and it was so much the worse for any limousine whose driver dared disobedience. The friendly, gum-chewing man at the wheel of our bus was as ruthless as the police. One gleaming Cadillac, slow at pulling in towards the sidewalk, was ricocheted cruelly into place by the front nearside wheel of our gargantuan coach. In high spirits, our driver jerked his head round and drawled:

"Say, that's five points for a Cadillac."

On we raced, flat out, till the escort sirened us to a full stop outside City Hall.

New York's Mayor kept us waiting ninety minutes, but when he eventually arrived, breezily and with great hustle, he proved to be a jolly personality whose immediate chief ambition was:

"Say, how's about getting my picture taken with the girls?"

And so we, the girls, joined him for a pose in the accepted style. With me were my friends, Carol Durand and Shirley Thomas, the Canadian show jumper with whom I was later to make a motor tour of the Eastern states.

That night we began the show in Madison Square Garden, the great Madison Square where all was hustle —but where the amenities were atrocious. Outside the show ring was a single small passage jammed at various times with saddle horses and harness ponies, international show jumpers and Canadian Mounties (who gave a spectacular display during the show), and with tractors and trailers stacked high with fences and equipment for the course. Incredible though it seemed, the "Garden" was bankrupt for space. Stabling was bad—stuffy as a night club—and many of the horses became listless, living virtually underground. We were luckier than other teams, for our horses were housed next to those of the Mounties in a tent which was cold but at least packed with fresh air as well as animals. Worst of all, however, was the fact that we had nowhere to exercise them, a shortcoming which largely accounted for a low standard of jumping throughout the competitions. Like athletes, horses need limbering-up before a performance, and consistent work for them is essential if they are to become receptive, responsive, and obedient. Hal and Tosca require an unusual amount of work—but in common with the others they were compelled to ride cold into the New York ring without even the advantage of a walk or a jog to warm them up. Inside the ring, arc lamps sent down a mild inferno of heat and glare.

The British team, despite these woeful conditions, went well, each of our riders winning an event. Tosca came back to form in time to join Prince Hal in the important President of Mexico Trophy contest. This above all was the prize I longed to win, though I felt my chances to be hopeless after I had dashed out during an interval to see an emotional film which left me feeling like a wet rag. Luckily, the tears of screen drama meant nothing to Hal and Tosca, and I had only myself to blame when between them they touched three fences. But when the points were finally totted up, the President of Mexico Trophy was mine. It is, I suppose, the prize I treasure more than any other—a finely wrought creation in Mexican silver showing a mounted cowboy about to throw a bull by twisting its tail.

In the space of three nights of fast-moving leisure we attended a glittering horse-show ball; a variety of night clubs, fashionable and otherwise; the fantastic entertainment world called Radio City where for a dollar and fifty cents we bought a film show, a ballet, revue numbers, a good symphony orchestra, a first-rate jazz band; and the Schubert Theatre. Among our evening visitors at the show was Sarah Churchill, the Premier's daughter, who had already become a major success in American television. I also toured the gigantic United Nations building, lunched among the babel of languages in its restaurant overlooking the river, attended two U.N.O. conferences, went to the Press stand where I was given a pair of earphones, switched rapidly from English to French, Spanish, Russian, and Chinese translations of one man's speech, and finally visited the interpreters' boxes to hear them translating, with impressive speed and fluency, while the delegate spoke.

Then New York became semi-paralysed by a week-end freak snow-storm. Traffic piled up, city dwellers slithered to and fro, and the big international horse race due to be run at Laurel Park, near Washington—with horses specially flown from England, France, and other countries —was postponed; this, however, was a lucky break for us, since the race was put back to the day after our show ended, which meant that we could fly out to Washington to watch it. On arrival, I was shown the imposing new course with glass-fronted stands where you dined, drank, and placed your bets almost without stirring from your seat. I was also given a fascinating close-up of the special starting gates by Eddie Blind, the country's ace starter. His job is a surprisingly specialized affair, for although

the mechanized gates look infallible, the horses may
nevertheless get off to a bad start unless the man in charge
ensures that the animals are all perfectly balanced. Eddie
pointed out to me the gang of small coloured boys poised
behind the horses in their gates.

"What are the little black boys for?" I asked.

"To pull the horse's tail up!" said Eddie.

Eddie went on to explain that it was vital to prevent a
horse from sitting down or working his way under the
rear of the pen. Before he could say another word I
got a practical demonstration of what he meant. Pointing to the gates, he yelled:

"Tail No. 13! Tail No. 13!"

And behind No. 13 pen the little black boy in blue
jeans and a multi-coloured shirt sprang into action,
made a grab at the tail of a handsome chestnut and
pulled it firmly upwards until the horse moved into
position.

Racecourse precautions against crooked riding or
other fraudulent practices were brought to a fine point at
Laurel Park; frequent saliva and blood tests were made,
but the choicest refinement was the filming machinery—
almost a studio—with four cameras set up on the track,
strategically sited to film the entire race. If any point
were in dispute, or a jockey suspected of unfair riding,
the stewards would call for the film (which got rapid
processing), start up the projector in the racecourse
"movie house", run through the race, and if necessary
call the jockey or jockeys concerned to view the show
for themselves—a visit to the movies they would doubtless prefer to miss. The international race we had come
to watch turned out to be a walk-over for the French

horse Worden, who for some extraordinary reason was allowed to start at the high price of 16 to 1.

Back in New York I was packing for Toronto, the last of our three show-jumping cities, when the telephone rang. A pleasant American voice said:

"Say, Pat—this is your cousin Ralph."

"Ralph—who?" I asked.

"Beermann, Ralph Beermann, your cousin."

Doubtfully I said "Oh yes," convinced I had never heard of the man, but knowing that I possessed several American relatives about whose family links I had never been clear. Unshaken by my coldness the amiable Mr. Beermann informed me that he and his family lived in Nebraska, and they would like it fine, he said, if they could have me visit with them.

I left things distinctly unsettled with Mr. B., and told Harry Llewellyn about the call. Harry was rudely intimidating.

"Your cousin, eh?" he taunted. "You'd better be careful, young woman—don't forget this is America. I'd check on my family tree if I were you." My innocent faith in human integrity thus shattered, I made some inquiries and had faith restored by the discovery that Mr. B. was indeed a cousin; we were to meet again before long. Meanwhile, we had the show jumping in Canada —at Toronto's Winter Fair, where the horses were beginning to feel the strain of nearly four weeks' concentrated effort. Conditions were easier at Toronto, fortunately, with a special exercising ground apart from the huge show ring; the most exciting contest was the puissance event which ended in a tie between America's Mrs. Carol Durand on Reno Kirk (a gallant nineteen-year-old) and Shirley Thomas riding Canada's powerful thoroughbred, White Sable. Harry Llewellyn, Bill Hanson, and I were delighted when Foxhunter, Prince Hal, and The Monarch carried off the Nations' Cup championship for Great Britain. The show ended in scintillating style with the ring full of cattle, prize-winning horses, and a team of square-dancing champions on a flower-decked wagon in the centre of the arena. That night, at a farewell celebration party, I filched from the buffet a placard which I pinned surreptitiously to the back of an American rival. In bold type, the card announced:

Assorted Tarts: 15 Cents a Package.

But our American friends got their revenge at midnight. It was 22 November, my twenty-fifth birthday, and with a great show of gallantry the U.S. team presented me with a gift—a gesture which moved me to a sense of shame for my prank an hour earlier.

I unwrapped the parcel and took out a book entitled *How to Clean up on Horses.* Inside was the picture of a wheelbarrow and a shovel.

Another diversion was the cocktail party held in Mr. E. P. Taylor's stables at the Winfield Stud. The drinks and snacks were served in the middle of a horse barn, so that guests could combine the social round, as it were, with first-hand inspection of fine stallions and thoroughbreds of all kinds. Beside one stall I stood admiring a lovely chestnut horse; suddenly he gave a flick of the tail and neatly lassoed my champagne glass by the stem. Next day we went to Niagara Falls, that haven of tourists and honeymooners, donned the regulation mackintoshes and gumboots, and stood in the strange tunnel behind the thundering cataract, gazing in awe through the water. When I heard that the pinnacle of General Brock's monument provided an amazing panorama of all Niagara, I insisted on climbing its 235 stone steps; perhaps the height was what did it, but whatever the reason I was reminded on the way down of Switzerland, and at once became inspired to yodel lustily; when I reached the bottom, the attendant clapped his hands, said "That sure was a great performance, lady" . . . and handed back my fifty cents admission fee.

A hilarious game had to be enacted when I visited the American side of the Falls. I had forgotten to bring my passport, and the frontier officer looked at me with solid suspicion. "Aren't you English?" he snapped.

I decided there was nothing for it but to join the Commonwealth. "No, I'm Canadian," I drawled.

"Where you from?" he said, his eyes glinting in the hope that I would be trapped.

I remembered the map, scorned the obvious cities like Ottawa or Toronto, and lied glibly:

"Just across the water. Oshawa." My Canadian accent shone, I thought.

He tried again. "Oh, yeah! I bet you've never bin near Oshawa."

I became indignant. "Hey, are you tryin' to make me out a liar?" I said. "I've lived aroun' Oshawa and Whitby and Newcastle for twenny years."

It worked. My recollection of English place-names on the map of Canada satisfied the official, though whether he was wholly convinced I was never certain.

The days and weeks that followed brought journeys by car, plane, bus and horse—ten thousand miles from the eastern end of Canada to the south-west tip of Texas on the borders of Mexico. I made ninety new friends and acquaintances; received all that is best in the goodwill pattern of American hospitality; went hunting; travelled in Kentucky, Florida, Nebraska, Colorado, Texas, and Kansas; watched a breathtaking rodeo near the broad sweep of the Rocky Mountains, with cowboys bareback-riding Brahma bulls in a display that outshone the wildest of Wild West fiction dramas; shot my own movies in settings of unutterable beauty; and ended with the ten most exciting days of my life on a million-acre ranch near the place where the Rio Grande sweeps down to the great Mexican Gulf.

It all began when the show jumping ended. With Shirley Thomas, I toured the eastern states from Canada south to Savannah in Georgia, on to Miami and along the Florida coast. With Shirley, too, I air-taxied back to Ottawa for Christmas. I won the horn-blowing competition, with an atrocious performance, at Ottawa's Hunt Ball. On New Year's Eve I dined in Rockford, Illinois, fifty miles west of Chicago—with a plateful of roast beef and Yorkshire pudding. I drank my champagne toast to 1954 beside the northern waters of the Mississippi (a thousand miles from where the old river of jazz-band steamboats flows past New Orleans). I shot a horned hoot-owl out west in Texas, hunted the fox back east in Virginia, and searched for trinkets in Syracuse. With Ralph, my cousin, I flew across rich corn lands and empty deserts, in the sun, in the darkness, in fog, rain, and icy wind. I sweated on the dusty prairie and shivered in the mountains. I rode a yellow mustang through ten hours of a Texas day. I drank thick, scalding coffee from a saucer on the ranch and sipped cool Martinis in the city. I met four millionaires with gold rings on their fingers, trouble on their minds; Mexican peasants with holes in their shirts, sun in their veins; and hard-riding cowboys with cattle to tame and songs to sing.

Back in England, friends would ask: "Did you enjoy your trip?"—to which I would reply: "Yes, it was lovely, thanks" . . . and as those weeks of high experience flashed through the mind's eye, I thought: How odd—to sum it all up with the polite formalities of suburban good manners.

CHAPTER 12

WATCHILY! WATCHILY!

LIKE a pocket kingdom—and not so small at that—
the King Ranch has a salty façade on the Mexican Gulf,
a pair of natural frontiers in the shape of the Rio Grande
River to the south-west, the Nueces to the north, and
a broad back door with one end leading to the rest of
Texas and the other to the mountains of New Mexico.
A million acres, give or take a few, carrying seventy-five
thousand head of cattle in a good year, but after four years
of drought, only fifty thousand by the time I reached the
ranch house near the end of January 1954.

From his home in Nebraska, my cousin Ralph flew me
south to Texas in his fast, new Bonanza plane; we
covered a thousand miles in six hours, and this was the
last of a hundred examples of Ralph Beermann's hospitality since the day his sudden phone call had come to
my New York hotel bedroom. I had stayed with Ralph
and his wife, Marjorie, at their home in Sioux City; had
been regally entertained by the entire family and most
of its friends; had been interviewed by Press and radio
men; had seen stock yards, wrestling matches and enough
inch-thick fillet steaks to fill a horse-box; and at Lincoln,
the State capital, had even met the Governor himself—
breezy Bob Crosby, who had launched a taxpayer's
Honesty Campaign ("everybody has to disclose exactly

what he's worth, now me, for instance, I'm worth six hundred dollars"). The Governor, who wore a handsome ruby ring, had earlier conducted me around rooms in the Capitol building. Proudly he indicated some of its treasures. "Just look at those tapestries," he said. "They'll last a lifetime."

Now, Ralph was piloting me south over Kansas, across the Red River and down to the Gulf for my ten wonderful days of work on the ranch. After miles of desolate prairie, dotted every now and then with an oil well, and pipe lines carrying natural gas across the land, we came upon the great King Ranch out of a low cloud. There it lay, a township in its own right, the main ranch house with a tall tower, white painted huts, barns, stables —and a race track.

The air strip was a field where horses halted their grazing to glance at the sky as we circled low in the hope that our noise would scatter them. But aeroplanes were no new sight for these placid ponies; they all held their ground and went on eating. We circled six or seven times before finding a gap long and wide enough to land safely. Watched by horses, Ralph taxied towards the ranch house where we climbed out of the elegant Bonanza and walked into a spacious courtyard that reminded me architecturally of a hundred places I had seen in Spain.

My hosts at King Ranch were genial Bob Kleberg and his wife, Helen. Like most of his employees, Bob talked about his work, and I was certainly an eager listener. By way of easy introduction I was shown the horses in training and taken to see the nearest cattle, which included three gigantic steers, five-year-olds, each weighing two hundredweight over a ton. King Ranch, I soon learned, was no mere farm—rather a major industry; it was divided into four main parts. Chief among these was the lovely headquarters of the ranch house, surrounded by palms, near a small creek from which the division took its name: the Santa Gertrudis Ranch; fine cattle, resistant to drought and ticks, had been bred here for thirty years. Then, miles away, lay the vast Norias Division, partly devoted to wild game, live oak, and cattle, partly typical prairie land carrying mesquite, prickly pear, and wild grasses. Third in the ranch hierarchy was Encino Division, all cattle country with mesquite and prickly pear abounding. Fourth was the Lorellis Division, lying on the Gulf between the towns of Kingsville and Corpus Christi. Until America claimed the Rio Grande as their border, much of the land had been Spanish—but that was a hundred years before, when a certain Captain King, after fighting in the Mexican war, founded the ranch which by the 1950's required a jeep trek of seventy miles when the boss went from his ranch house out to Norias.

For me, next morning, Norias was the scene of my first day's work—but not before Helen had taken me into Kingsville to buy buckskin chaps. . . . "You can't be comfortable riding cowboy style without chaps," they had said. That day, too, Ralph Beermann climbed aboard his Bonanza and flew home to Nebraska; to him I largely owed the pleasures and thrills that were to follow.

Bob and I got into the station wagon and set off on the ninety-minute drive to Norias, off the road and across the rail track, over the prairie for another few miles, until out of the January morning mist loomed a perfectly delightful scene. It was a prairie cookhouse with a shaded eating place.

Open fires licked the dust in the air; low barricade fences cut off one section from another, and to one side was a roof of tarpaulins supported by poles, where trestle tables were being laid for lunch—knife, fork, spoon, mug. The fires were for cooking, and the chefs were Mexicans.

It was nine-thirty when Bob and I arrived; the sun's heat was beginning to clear the mist which had drifted in from the sea, and when we pulled up alongside the cookhouse, a dark-tanned Mexican walked out with two mugs of strong coffee. I sat, sipping my brew in the station wagon, gazing around me. A moment later there was a great yelling and pounding of hooves. A red calf streaked past the wagon; then a cowboy, galloping in noisy chase, pulled up his mustang outside the cookhouse door, swirled a lariat, and with a brilliant throw roped the racing calf twenty feet ahead. The Mexican cook immediately ran from his kitchen, flashed a butcher's knife, killed the calf and began hauling it towards the fence. Three hours later, when we returned for lunch, the calf skin lay drying in the sun while five kinds of veal, freshly cut, had been fried, roasted, or casseroled on the open fires.

Bob and I drove out to the herd, which on this part of the prairie consisted of five to six hundred head of mixed cattle in the charge of ten Mexican cowboys. Each ranch division had its own cowboy "outfit". But apart from the regular cowboys there were also the small hordes of Mexican "wetbacks"—ragged though happy prairie labourers who tramped across the Rio Grande from Mexico, mile after mile through the mesquite, smuggling their way past the frontier guards—all for an odd job on the ranch, to earn a dollar or two, buy a shirt, then hike back to their families until the next time. On the ranch they shouted, worked excitedly, got in everybody's path—but earned themselves a dollar a day and food.

Bob sent for our horses. Mine was a yellow mustang, pale in colour but bright in spirit. The saddle was a Western type with a high pommel to hold the strain of a lasso, and the stirrups were long, to ease the strain of a long day on horseback. I was wearing my jeans, buckskin chaps, coloured check shirt, and Western hat; for a while I just sat on the mustang, watching the wild, exciting operation called "cutting out" cattle.

"Cutting out" is simply the separation of various types of cattle from the rest of the herd. First they set aside the poor quality cows; then the range bulls, not quite up to top standard; then weedy, crippled, or otherwise irregular calves; then the best bulls; then the yearling calves. These weanlings go to another part of the ranch for fattening, and thence to the nation's meat markets. All try violently to evade being "cut out" and to outwit the horseman by worming back to the mixed-up safety of the herd. A cow or calf that escapes once, becomes more cunning when the rider tries cutting it out a second time. But the Mexicans and their horses were fast, brave, and highly skilled; so were Bob Kleberg and his leading hands. Whatever the size of the herd, they could fix an eye on a bull, calf, or cow, ride into the tightly packed mass of cattle, and head off their chosen beast with an uncanny technique. The pace was backbreaking, the noise of men and cattle rose to a crescendo of whooping and bellowing, while the dust flew as the hooves pounded the earth. I was entranced by the whole scene. I was also shaken out of theoretical study of the problem by Bob's voice:

"You've bin sittin' there long enough, Pat. How about gettin' to work?"

Then he introduced me to my partner for the day, tough, broad, middle-aged Ed Durham, a man with humour and kindness in his sun-wrinkled face. Ed proceeded to teach me two-thirds of the little I learned about the art of cutting cattle, and my horse taught me the rest; these prairie mounts were so fast that they could twist the spirit out of any cow intent on escaping the chase.

As I rode forward with Ed, I knew that many eyes were upon me—those of the Mexican "Pick-up boys" who stayed close to the herd, as well as the division Bosses who had been cutting out calves. There was no mockery in the frank stares, merely a calm interested hint of impending disaster for the green girl who asked so many questions. I knew that every move I made was being given close scrutiny; the critical eyes noted how I sat, how I reined, how I turned—in short, how much of a rider was this English senorita. If I failed in the next hour, I might as well quit, for I was not interested in being treated as some odd variety of lady tourist, with amused tolerance; at cutting out, I wanted desperately to do an honest job.

So into the herd I went. "See that painted calf," Ed had said, pointing to an easily-placed one. "Try getting *him* out."

It was hotter now, and dustier, and the cows were

(*Above*) Tosca jumping at the White City

(*Right*) Prince Hal winning the Gloucestershire Area International Trial at Badminton, May 1955

Schooling Prince Hal (*above*) and Mr. Hanson's
Flanagan (*below*) at Miserden

kicking up an awful racket as they got separated from their calves. For a moment my yearling was lost in the jostling movement of the herd, but then I picked him out again, about fifteen yards away, and decided on a simple outflanking ploy. Suddenly he stopped, turned, and looked right at me as my yellow mustang came within six feet; then the yearling gave a snort and a wriggle, lowered his head and charged off to the left of me. At once the mustang was after him. By a lucky chance my yearling cooked his own goose, for the evading dash had sent him to the brink of the herd and it was the work of a minute to edge him slowly, twisting, turning all the way, out into the open. For a hundred yards I chased him at a gallop, then managed to turn him out to the Pick-up boys. The job was done, and, nonchalantly, I walked my horse back into the herd where Ed and Bob, rocking in their saddles, were laughing their heads off. But thank heaven, it was the laughter of approval.

"For a beginner, that was just fine—for a beginner," said Bob, and I began dreaming that London was some far-off city with not much interest, come to think of it, for us riders of the Texas range. But then my horse predicted a calf's movements quicker than I had, and I nearly fell off. So I sobered up.

We worked our horses in half-hour shifts, which was about all they could take of these gruelling operations. Thirty minutes' cutting out, then thirty minutes' rest—while a cowboy roped fresh mounts from the Ramuda, the herd of horses a half-mile away, where each man had three or four to ride alternately in the relays of work.

Lunch was served in the shade of the cookhouse; we sat on long wooden benches at an unpretentious table;

there was fresh meat, plenty of beans, and always the strong coffee; it was, in fact, a polite tradition never to ride past the cookhouse at any time of day without pausing for a mouthful of coffee. I noticed, too, that these cowboys drank heavily—not rye whisky or other hard liquors in the two-gun tradition of saloon fiction, but *milk*. "Sure, we like liquor," said one—"in moderation, just like most other folks. But milk—now there's a great drink for a hot day's riding." And away he walked for forty-five minutes' *siesta* before getting back to work. It was enough to break the heart of any small boy with a picture in his mind of the pistol-packing Wild West.

At the end of a week's work with the ranch hands I felt I was just one of the crowd. Riding in and around the herd, I learned a few of the orders, shouted in Spanish mixed queerly with English; the Mexicans would often refer to *el highway*, and for the warning, "Look out!" would call: "Watchily, watchily!"

Before long, my most devoted friend was Adán Muñoz, a dark, humorous young Mexican who could rope a calf with the best of them. During the two days working at Norias I went with Adán, Bob, Ed Durham, and the others twice a day to the prairie stockyard two miles away. Here we brought that section of the herd which had been cut out. On these treks a steer roped by the horns was used as a leader; one cowboy rode ahead, leading a specially-trained steer so that an arrowhead could be formed, behind which the rest of us could drive forward the cows, bulls, and calves taken from the herd. At the stockyard, where the dust flew yet more thickly, we sorted the cattle out, ran them into chutes that led to their pens, and helped the reluctant ones with a push and a yell. Several cowboys carried small electrically-charged "prodders" which helped to speed the operation; occasionally, there seemed to be just the faintest hint of enjoyment in this mild infliction of cruelty by the men.

On one of our journeys to the stockyard I was allowed to take the lead steer, riding out in front, pulling on the rope, with the herd behind me. But this was a gesture to give me the feel of it all; for a novice it would have been impossible to lead the arrowhead of tramping cattle more than a short distance, since the prairie was flat and directionless, and unless you were expertly intimate with each clump of scrub or mesquite, you would hardly know, except for the sun, where you were heading.

Each evening, out on the prairie, I saw the young calves branded—first across the ribs with the famous running W of the King Ranch, then lip-branded. Bull calves were castrated, and this was a performance accompanied by a boisterous, fantastic sport in which little Mexican boys—some mere five-year-olds—ran about with small pouches into which they placed the testicles of treated calves: a delicacy for dinner among Mexican families, I learned. For the branding, large fires were built; then Adán, Bob Kleberg, and Ed Durham began roping the calves, neatly lassoing the head or a leg, so that Mexican "wetbacks" could tie down the animal near to the fire where branding irons were being heated. Awesome, too, were the sight and sounds of a saw grating through the fabric of a cow's horns—which had to be sawn-off if they were ingrowing; the severing of each horn took only a minute.

Just before sunset we stopped work. I looked into the

sky to watch huge V-formations of thousands of geese flying home to some inland lake. An hour later, driving back to the ranch house, I heard wild turkeys gobbling in the darkness, and saw deer silhouetted against the skyline on a hump of high land. I slept well that night.

Next day we went to work on the Encino Division, forty miles away, cutting out a larger herd of nearly a thousand cattle. On this part of the ranch I met Humphrey, the arch clown among cowboys. A friend of the Durhams and Klebergs, Humphrey had come to the ranch for a spell of cutting out and to get what he called his annual exercise. Full of banter, blarney, and mock heroics, his antics tended occasionally to bring a kind of gay chaos into the work. While cutting out, Humphrey seemed to lose as many calves as he found; and since they escaped him so often, even the dullest calf contrived enough cunning to reduce Humphrey to a state of helplessness. The day's biggest joke was a tale spread widely among the men by the youthful Adán. I had complained to Adán (ran the story) that Humphrey was the worst "pardner" I had ever worked with in all my experience of cutting cattle. There were many similar hilarious diversions, not the least of which was Humphrey's constant effort to "star" in all the movies I shot, between and during work periods, with my small ciné camera.

Humphrey, however, was not the only cowhand who failed, so to speak, to get his calf. During the afternoon a diminutive and exceptionally agile calf had escaped him four or five times. With a great show of pretended annoyance Ed Durham and I decided to go after the calf ourselves, after telling Humphrey he was fired. Entering into the spirit of the thing, Humphrey looked crestfallen and waited for us to show him how "experts" went to work. By this time the calf had gone nimbly to the centre of the herd. But Ed and I were watching it all the time and we called out almost in unison:

"It's O.K., Ed, I've got my eye on him."

"It's O.K., Pat, I've got my eye on him."

Then, from different directions, Ed and I rode into the rumbling mass of a thousand cattle.

Our grand strategy, unhappily, did not work out as planned. I had *my* eye on the calf, all right; and Ed had *his* eye on the calf, all right. The trouble was—we had those eyes on different calves. As we charged amid clouds of dust towards the edge of the herd, we collided with each other, while Humphrey's elusive creature pounded its way to freedom. A triumphant cry went up from the Mexicans. "Olé! Olé! Olé!" they jeered.

"So that's how it's done!" yelled Humphrey. And blushing with shame, Ed and I pretended not to hear.

I was supremely happy. But now we were into February, and I began counting the hours before this strange, exciting life of the prairie closed down. Early next morning, with Sam Chesshire, the local doctor, and José, a young Mexican, I toured in an open car through lovely pasture lands, dense brush, and across the vast game reserve to the sea. Less than a mile from the salt Mexican Gulf were fresh-water lakes covered with duck and geese in unbelievable thousands. We saw lovebirds, wild turkey, and javelin, the little wild boars; and on the homeward journey I shot my horned hoot-owl.

José saw it first, as we drove through the brush away

197

from the salt marshes near the Gulf. The large owl sat motionless. José stopped the car, reached for the .22 rifle in a scabbard running down the side of the door, and handed it to me.

"Want to try your luck?" he asked.

I took the gun and aimed. The big horned owl was nearly a hundred yards away.

Although, as it happens, I am not a bad shot, I would not care to assess the percentage of luck with this one. Say ninety-five. But lucky or not, I got him—first shot. José and the doctor were astounded, and looked at me with an entirely new, respectful awe. Complacently I examined my nails, and handed back the .22 with a smile. Then we drove home.

In the evening I talked with Louis Lundean, the American painter, who was on a visit to the ranch. His sketches and water colours—of cockerels, of peacocks roaming the ranch house lawn, of landscapes and horses, of the dusty prairie, of cattle cutting, roping, and branding—were delicate and inspired. He had also painted a sketch of me—on a cutting horse.

Four days later I was back in England, and four hours after landing at London Airport I was broadcasting on "In Town Tonight," alongside a ballerina, a cowboy, and the British actor Jack Hawkins. Then I went home to Miserden.

I unwrapped the most treasured of all my souvenirs—the Lundean painting. I hung it on the long wall of my Miserden entrance hall, stepped a yard back, and gazed at it for a quarter of an hour.

At the end of which time the sketch became crowded with the misty shapes of men and cattle and horses . . .

Adán and the yellow mustang; Bob Kleberg and Ed Durham; José, Sam Chesshire, the clowning Humphrey; the Mexican cook and a score of Mexican wetbacks; a herd of fifty thousand cattle; and a gang of cowhands drinking coffee beside a cookhouse on the Texas prairie.

CHAPTER 13

BOOTS, BRAN, AND BREECHES . . .

A SHOW JUMPER'S BUDGET

IT IS, as the old cliché puts it, a great life if you don't weaken. Given a constitution robust enough to support four hours' travel, all-day and all-evening show jumping, midnight supper and a two a.m. party, followed by a hundred-mile drive home in the horsebox—and still be in time for early morning service on a Sunday—there is indeed no reason for weakening, especially at the age of twenty-six. And although I adore the flurry, the crowds of the big shows and the trips to Spain, Switzerland, France, Italy, and the U.S.A., there are moments when I am quite ready to leave the highlights and to look forward to the September season of small local shows within reasonable distance of home. This is the time when only greyhounds and athletic young men are leaping at the White City; when the great occasions of summer show jumping are ended and the international Harringay is still just a name on an entry form. This is the time when I drive Prince Hal and Tosca away from Miserden for a quiet country round of show jumping that does not make newspaper headlines; not, at least, in any Press more sensation-seeking than a Cotswold weekly or a Welsh mountain clarion. This is the time when Tosca, Hal, and I are jogging to the little places like Senny

Bridge, for a peaceful show run by the Devynock Agricultural Society, or the Blackwood show of the Bedwellty people, or the St. Mellons events, or the jumping in tranquil Carmarthen.

Even these rural excursions bring unexpected drama. One day, driving the jeep with a two-wheel trailer in tow, a tyre swelled to bursting point, went off with a bang that jolted the neighbourhood, and stranded me with two startled horses and a jumping competition an hour ahead. I had never before tried hitch-hiking with horses. But the three of us thumbed a lift for twenty miles that day, in a truck which bore a label saying "Horse Meat, Unfit for Human Consumption."

Too soon, however, our gipsy wanderings are over, and the hurrying tension of an international horse show is with us again. I have always suspected that the growing audiences of show jumping possess little or no notion of the labour and patience which ends under the arc lamps with a neat-coated figure on horseback, jumping (or hitting) a six-barred gate in the competitive arena. Let me therefore try to sketch the blue-print for an international competition.

I make up my mind about which events I shall enter some six or eight weeks before the show. Each event will cost £1, sometimes £2, and since I can never know whether Hal or Tosca will be fit and sound "on the night," I must take a chance on this initial outlay. For the White City Show, in mid-July, I complete my arrangements towards the end of May. A week before the opening I must ensure that the horses are in first-class condition; perhaps one needs a little tonic, the other something extra in the feed. On the Saturday before the show, Pauline and I load up the horsebox and drive to London; we resemble a travelling circus, for into the horsebox, aside from us and the horses, goes a fantastic array of equipment and medicaments.

Enough hay for a week or ten days; oats, chaff, and bran; linseed oil and a large medicine chest containing anti-phlogistine, animal lintex, straps and bandages, hoof oil, and a variety of other lotions and embrocations. For mere quantity, this is the least of it; the tack must be organized as if we were a cavalry regiment bound for an overseas duty tour.

Bridles and saddles, and spares in case either get lost or damaged; rugs for the horses when they're indoors, and mackintosh sheets for when it rains, which is often; soap for the saddlery, polish for my boots; bedding for the groom, Pauline, who sleeps in the horsebox—and, therefore, food for the groom, which also means a gas ring so that she can cook in the box, thus adding sauce-pans, kettle, cups, plates, cutlery, butter, sugar, bacon, cornflakes, three tins of coffee, half a pound of tea, and salt (which we invariably forget).

Horses also need boots and goloshes, and studs to prevent slipping while they jump. Leg bandages for while they travel, and tail guards to prevent chafing. Hay nets, to prevent waste, and buckets for water. Straw in the box, for comfort and safety.

Then comes the small matter of *my* equipment. Trivial —for all I need is breeches, boots, spurs, coat (and spare coats), hacking jacket, shirts, stocks, gloves, hunting cap, whips, toothbrush, cosmetics, outdoor clothes and nylons, pyjamas, and underwear. To these I add the impedimenta of show jumping social events—a cocktail dress, an evening dress, a day dress, the shoes and bags to accompany each, plus a hat that looks reasonable, for formal occasions.

Then we drive to White City, a hundred miles in four hours, fully loaded and with a pause for water. On a Saturday afternoon it is almost certain that I must cope with a Press interview, a TV appearance, or a radio recording, or all three. But that day and on Sunday, too, the horses must be worked hard to stop them becoming too fresh and disobedient.

Monday dawns and I rise at six-thirty. I am staying with a friend not far from central London—but jumping often starts at nine o'clock and I must reach White City by eight in order to look around the course, learn my order of jumping, and, probably, write four or five post-cards over a cup of tea. Long before entering the ring to compete, I must "ride in" the horses to make them supple and receptive, for the excitement of coming to London is unsettling—even with a horse. Then, some five horses before our own turn, we are called to the inner collecting ring, where we walk about on the peat surface, pretending to be very cool and confident. When our number comes up, Paul quickly cleans the peat from the horse's studs, and into the show ring we ride. We have, we hope, memorized the direction, order, and nature of eighteen or twenty fences. And so to the jumps.

After a brilliant—or, as the case may be, awful, indifferent, disastrous, or merely infuriating—round, we come from the ring and go to be weighed like any jockey of the race track; if we have done well, we wait for the jump-off against other competitors who pass the early stages, or the finals, or maybe march to the centre of the ring to receive a rosette if we're lucky. Then the horse cools off and goes back to the temporary stable. But at White City's international shows there are morning, afternoon, and evening sessions; with two or three horses, you may be jumping from nine in the morning until eleven at night—and I frequently am. An official party may follow and I get to bed at two, rise at seven, reach the White City by eight-thirty and start a new day in the show ring; there is not much time for daydreaming.

As for the horses, the qualities of character which must be fostered all the time are their courage, confidence, and calmness. Once a horse has reached international status, the courage is there for all to see; but calmness and confidence are things that must be nurtured. A horse will jump calmly if it is not over-anxious, or frightened, or lacking confidence in the rider; and, of course, a naturally excitable animal, like Prince Hal, needs a great quantity of schooling and obedience training, until he knows that jumping is all in the day's work. Hal and Tosca absorbed the lesson long ago, but not without struggle and anxiety.

Good show jumpers, like good athletes, love jumping, and those with the rare, brave qualities that lead to the top of their world, usually have the temperament to go with it all. For me, one of the most profitable and fascinating experiences has been to live alongside the strikingly different characters of Hal and Tosca, and to observe the processes through which one—Tosca—has found her element jumping in the open air, and the other —Hal—reaches his highest peaks on the courses of the indoor arena.

Why is Prince Hal an indoor character, and Tosca an outdoor girl? It is a question of their different veins of boldness. Hal, the excitable thoroughbred, has tremendous natural impulsion and an almost libertine boldness. He demands freedom and the right to assume complete control. But these he must not be allowed, and thus a valuable paradox is created; difficult to control, hemmed in by the limited spaces and the solid walls of the indoor ring, Hal acquires a sense of discipline—without losing his natural daring. His boldness soars. And so, indoors —the bolder the horse, the better he jumps. Tosca, on the other hand, is ultra-careful, hates touching a fence, and on the indoor course often becomes over-anxious— thus losing her *"joie de vivre."* In the open air, however, Tosca usually offers me total obedience, and so marshals herself that I can take her with deadly accuracy to all her fences.

One of my chief difficulties at Miserden is that I do not own a single square foot of land, and must therefore rely for my paddock facilities upon local farmers and the landlord. Few people have fields to spare, even for renting, and I am unable to construct the track, jumping lane, ditches, and water jumps which would be invaluable for training and practice. Photographers and journalists, visiting me at Miserden, have usually said: "Now, I'd like to see your paddock and jumps." Then they walk alongside while I ride the horses to a pleasant stone-walled field behind the village, and are shocked by the sight of my collection of old pine poles, resting on tar barrels or oil drums. Some suspect that I possess a finely equipped dream of a paddock hidden around the corner. I do. But it remains a dream.

A show jumper's budget is a complex affair at Miserden, for we are not only landless, but lack even adequate storage space. This means that I must buy, month by month at the prevailing market price, every scrap of feed and domestic paraphernalia required in my stables: hay, oats, bran, straw, horse nuts, linseed oil, and a score of other items, not to mention saddlery and similar equipment. In winter and early spring, the hay alone may cost from £15 to £20 a ton. The horses tend to eat one ton a week. Oats at thirty shillings a hundredweight and bran at forty-five per sack is also eaten with a gay disregard of the financial consequences.

My own shoes are cheaper than those of the horses; once a quarter comes a blacksmith's bill of anything from £15 to £25. Insurance is vital; one can take risks with cheap horses. . . . But a Hal or Tosca is the find of a lifetime. Even so I could not afford to insure Tosca for more than two hundred pounds until 1953, when I raised the figure to two thousand. Add to this the fact that the horsebox swallows petrol at the rate of one gallon every ten miles and also that there is a substantial bill for repairs and maintenance.

On the other hand I can only represent Great Britain in the team if I am an amateur, and therefore I may never accept money personally for riding lessons or use my knowledge in a professional way. Even when I am invited to join the British team I have to consider quite simply whether I can afford it, because for every visit abroad I may miss twenty or more successful competitions at home with far less strain on the horses. Moreover, foreign competitions are not easily won.

Without the horses I would never have had an opportunity to travel, and to meet other people, for it is this mutual interest in horses that has given me the chance to make new friends abroad, rather than being suffered only as a tourist. Nationality makes very little difference between the members of the various teams, and I really enjoy trying to learn something about other countries and their languages. It is far more interesting staying with kind friends in a private house. Even when one has to stay at an hotel during the activities of a horse show one never gets the luxury of five minutes to oneself. Personally I find this quite a good thing, as perhaps I might lose any ability to make sociable conversation if I had more time to brood on the problems of the forthcoming event.

Anyway, one rarely gets much intelligent conversation out of a rider before a big competition, especially if he is concentrating on some of the necessary things such as his horse, the fences, the turns in the course, the adjustment of his saddlery, his number and general turnout. Likewise, can one blame the rider for turning the other way when some stranger pushes a grubby scrap of paper at him for an autograph?—for at that moment it is the rider's job to see that his or her horse is best prepared for the competition. It is part of his duty to the public to put up a good performance with his horse rather than with his signature!

One of the disadvantages of going abroad is the accumulation of work at home. I had quite a shock, which quickly brought me back to earth, when I returned from America. There were five large cardboard grocery boxes brimming over with unopened letters waiting in my room. These gave me the greatest pleasure to read, but meantime the horses were champing in the stables needing work. On top of this there were various social engagements which had to be fulfilled. The most impressive of these was the Presentation of the Sportsman and Sportswoman of the Year Trophy at the Savoy. I had stayed on in America for three months after the shows had finished there, travelling around remote places.

While I was away, I had not realized how well the Press had reported our successes during the autumn tour. From a complete lack of interest in our trials and errors of 1947 there had been very slight public attention in 1949, when the only headlines in the papers read, "English Lady Goes Wrong Way in Paris." This referred to someone taking the wrong course, merely because the horse chose his own route. There was no mention of one or two good British wins at that show. Interest was definitely stimulated by the Olympic Games. First the result at the closing ceremony at Wembley in 1948, when our team won the Bronze Medal in the Grand Prix des Nations. Then to that sensational moment in 1952 when we at home switched on our radio sets to hear the National Anthem being played on that final day at Helsinki. At once, we knew that the team had won the Gold Medal. This was in spite of the fact that the English had had their backs against the wall after the first disastrous round.

The wonderful effort of the people who sponsored our American venture in the autumn of 1953 was luckily well repaid. The Press had given great credit to Prince Hal's success in America. From Hal and Tosca's consistently good results, I found, to my surprise and pleasure, that I had been elected the Sportswoman of the Year. People were becoming more interested in the sport of show jumping.

At home I soon had to start training the horses for the jumping events at Badminton. The three-day event had already become very popular, with people coming to watch and bringing their cars and families from far counties. Combined training or *Concours Complet* as it is aptly called by the French, is the training necessary to produce the combination of the complete rider with the complete horse, able to cope with any situation or obstacle. The finished result takes much time and patience. Through the encouragement of combined training events at Badminton, Harewood and the many one-day events through the country, Britain now has a team of really good horses and riders. They are trained for this combination of a dressage test, cross-country and steeplechase, with show jumping on the third day. This last test is really to show that the horses are still supple and obedient after the rigours of the middle day.

At Badminton, after the jumping test has been carried out and the winner has been found for the whole of the three-day event, other ordinary show jumping competitions are held in the main ring. The most important of these was called the Badminton Grand Stakes. Prince Hal and Tosca were due to jump in this, but I had some difficulty in getting them to the show. To my concern, I found that Tosca had slightly lost her nerve for travelling. If she felt that she had not enough foot room in the lorry, she would scuffle her feet until she nearly slipped down. After a lot of patience, reloading with the horses in different partitions, and some extra smooth driving, Tosca settled down, and we arrived safely.

Princess Margaret was watching the competition from a wagon in the centre of the ring. My first round was on Prince Hal, the hero of the American tour. He was jumping in great style when, true to the saying that even the mighty fall, he stumbled as he landed over a fence and deposited me at the foot of the wagon. Tosca made amends for this by jumping superbly, and winning on the timed jump-off. She received her rosette and was petted by the Princess.

The horses then went straight over to Ireland where they commenced their international season at Cork Show. Tosca made a very good start by winning, although Prince Hal was rather excited and disobedient. The courses at this show were excellent, and I thought that these competitions would really restore Tosca's shaken confidence, caused by her two bad falls the year before. However, on the first night we had a competition with bad floodlighting, and this again upset her. The lighting was too low, and shone like headlights into the horses' eyes. They were blinded as they approached some fences, and other fences looked like ghostly shadows out of the arc of the lights. Although the next day she was brave enough to win the "An Tostal" Championship, and a big bronze shield, the fright that she had had when jumping in bad light showed its effect in Dublin. It was the first time I had ever jumped in this lovely arena, as I have always been too busy in August to compete at the Dublin Summer Show. I had been given quite a build-up before my first appearance at the Spring Show, and perhaps Tosca felt the strain of the occasion. We entered the ring with all the eyes of Dublin turned to watch our performance. Tosca was very hesitant over the first two fences, and then at the third, right in front of the Grand Stand, she suddenly stopped, and I slowly fell off. Our dignity was slightly redeemed when Prince Hal won another competition, and then Tosca became more confident before the end of the Show. The hospitality of the Irish is well known and indeed we had been royally entertained. It had been a happy addition to my memories of 1948. But with no time for reminiscences I had to rush back to England for the Oxford County Show.

For the first time, a British team was being sent to Portugal before going on to Madrid, where the Spanish were holding the World Championship. Along with Major Gibbon, Captain Dallas and Lady Mary Rose Williams, I had been invited with Prince Hal and Eforegiot. Eforegiot is a lovely bay horse, kindly lent to me by Miss Paget. In 1951 he had won the leading show jumper competition at Harringay, and he is the ideal type for international competitions. At home there were hectic preparations for this long trip abroad. Not only was Tosca being left behind, but also some young horses, whose training programme would be interrupted until my return.

Before the horses left England, Prince Hal won a test competition at Lambourn, a home of many racehorses. Then the horses called in at the Royal Windsor Show for one competition en route for the ship. Actually it was Tosca who won this competition, although Prince Hal had won it a year or so before. The international horses acquitted themselves satisfactorily, and I picked up my two from Windsor at crack of dawn the next morning. Unfortunately, the silencer on the lorry had succumbed to wear and tear, so I had to drive through the heart of London to the docks well heralded by the deafening reverberations of the engine. Even the horses objected to this and were battering the boards just behind my head with their hind hooves. I did not think that it was at all funny until I saw the business men in the city holding on to their bowlers and looking anxiously for the tank battalion that was presumably invading their domain. Once down at the docks, everyone was charming. We were shown around the ship, introduced to the stewards, and Prince Hal and Eforegiot were lucky enough to have the same crates that had been used for two royal polo ponies a week or so before.

Leaving my horses in the good care of Pauline, I went back to Windsor, and then on to Trowbridge Show where Tosca jumped in her best form, before being left in peace at Miserden.

Practically before Tosca had cooled down from her final round in Wiltshire, I was driving to London Airport to catch the Lisbon plane. It was exciting enough to be flying to Portugal for the first time, but the climax was to be in Spain, where the competition for the World Championship was being held.

After a great welcome at Lisbon Airport, we found our horses well stabled in a private yard near the Showground. Everyone was unbelievably helpful and charming, and I was in high spirits when we went that evening to the official show reception. After meeting our hosts, and all the foreign teams, I happened to be talking to a Spaniard. During the course of the conversation he casually remarked that of course I knew that ladies were not eligible for the World Championship

212

competition. My heart dropped into my party shoes. This event at Madrid was to be the climax and aim of the tour, and as far as I knew my entries had been accepted. Further questioning, frantic telephoning, despair, and then a general despondency followed. There was nothing to be done about it, as apparently some international rule had been passed, and we had not been informed. There was the consolation that my horses could jump in all the other events.

It was impossible to ignore the blessings for long, and the next morning, after we had worked the horses, and the sun was beginning to compensate for his shyness at home, Senhor Graça, the owner of the house and stables, came out to talk to us. We were invited to sit in the pleasant shade of the trees, and to taste a variety of his delicious wines. At the same time we could watch our horses being groomed and cooled off. The grooms were playing a hose of cold water on the horses' legs to refresh and strengthen them before the week's jumping. We also had to decide on the entries for each horse, but before long we had drifted from the technicalities of show jumping to the intriguing hobby of our host.

He had superb English greyhounds for coursing, and knew their pedigrees back to the original root of their family tree. I have a fellow-interest in greyhounds, as I had been given a young greyhound called Windy in 1950. Windy is a brindle bitch, with enough lurcher blood in her to become the most charming and attractive companion, an efficient and silent poacher, and yet a sentimental friend and housedog. So our conversation warmed with the description of our respective grey-hounds, and after we had seen the kennels we retired to the house to see photographs of the champion dogs. I was most intrigued by some of the tiled inside walls, showing pictures of hunting scenes or designs. Many of the good houses have outside tiling which, like a thatch, keeps the house cool in the summer and dry in the winter. The houses can be kept spotlessly clean with this practical and attractive architecture. The tiles are tough, and last for a long time. They do not need constant repair like an English thatch. For a thatch is made from essential material for birds' nests, and the birds will steal the straw unless the thatch is securely netted.

Lisbon is a charming place, built on many hills, like Rome. Looking out over the blue bay formed by the mouth of the River Tagus, one could see all the little sailing boats busy in the perpetual wind from the Atlantic. The Gulf Stream does not flow along the coast of Portugal, so I was alternately stimulated by bathing in the cold sea and baked by the hot sun. The controversy arose as to whether swimming affects one's judgment. If my eye was put out by springtime bathing under blue skies, the horses were not so affected. They both jumped brilliantly over the excellent and big international courses, and they both won. I think that Hal's "coup," the Six Bar competition, was for me more exciting than any other event so far.

It was held on a rather English evening, with grey clouds and drizzle. Hal had never before attempted this rather specialist competition in which one faces a line of six straight fences with only two strides between each. To give him an idea of what to do, we rigged up a practice line outside the arena. The first time we tried, Hal jumped the first two fences with feet to spare, but as he landed over the second the third fence blew down in front of him. He stopped in a flash, and my impetus carried me straight over his head. At that moment my number was called from the main ring, and I had to remount Prince Hal without a moment in which I could brush off the tell-tale sand from my hat. We rode into the ring. I was worried and Hal was upset. Somehow we coped with that line of fences, only just managing to put in the two strides between each. For Prince Hal was trying to gain speed, and I was trying to regain control. By the time the fences had been raised for the third jump-off we were at last in harmony. Prince Hal revelled in the final jump-off over three six-foot fences, and he knew he was wonderful as he cleared the last with inches to spare, just before dusk fell on that rare damp day in Portugal.

Not a moment's peace for sightseeing in this charming and hospitable country. Although one day I was taken for the one-hundred-mile drive to Fatima to see the new cathedral. This has just been finished with an impressive semicircular façade of pillars, built on the site of the miracle of thirty years ago. A vision of the Virgin Mary appeared to some children who were guarding their sheep and goats. Then a spring of water there was found to have some power of healing, as at Lourdes. I was impressed by the simplicity of the tiny chapel where the services are now held for the pilgrims, until the new cathedral is finished. In comparison, this modern cathedral is not nearly so attractive as the ornate stone work of the lovely old fourteenth-century cathedral at Batalha. Portugal is rich in historical palaces and interesting places, as well as the more modern holiday resorts such as Estoril with its flowered terraces, villas and casino.

We were entertained at the casino one night after the show, and I was shown the gambling-room with the people at the roulette tables. The players were very tense, and I saw one large lady perched on a stool, raking in the *escudos* with grim determination. I am sure that she did not enjoy her win as much as I had enjoyed Prince Hal's victory earlier that day!

I was also taken to a pinnacle of Lisbon, under the Moorish castle, where one looks down on the old part of the city, with its very narrow streets and unique style, almost reminiscent of the Kasbah in Algiers. Then a quick look at the fabulous collection of coaches, including one that an English queen had travelled in to Spain. This was not only superbly upholstered, with strong and efficient suspension and springing, all camouflaged with fabulously gilded figures, but it also had a modern convenience, which our guide took great pleasure in showing us!

All these glimpses of the wealth in art and history were seen by us "*toujours à la course*," freely translated as "always at the double." In fact, by eleven o'clock that same morning, we were already on the road for Madrid, chosen ground for the World Championship.

I was astounded at the speed and smoothness of the little "*4 chevaux*" in which we travelled. There were three riders and all their luggage piled into this tiny car, for a 450-mile drive over arid mountains and isolated country.

We passed through lonely villages, each with its church, and large, untidy stork's nest on the tower.

Perhaps this is the reason for all the small children we saw playing in the villages. I imagined I was back in medieval times when I saw the walled town of Avila, looking strongly secure from any barbaric attack. The effect of the mottled bronze of the ironstone, and the beautiful proportions of the inside of this cathedral gave me an impression of austere dignity. A feeling most fitting to the character of St. Teresa, who lived in Avila four hundred years ago.

Then on through the Gates of the Lions of Castile, and over the Guadarrama Mountains. Below us on the plains I could see the farms where the fighting bulls were bred, and I remembered three years before when I had held a cape myself.

The Madrid show ground had some new stables for the horses, and Prince Hal was in a comfortable box. He seemed to be pleased to be back in Spain, where he had performed in his first international show. He showed his pleasure by jumping with superb confidence, culminating in winning the Grand Prix.

I could hardly believe the result when it was announced that Hal was three seconds faster than any other clear round. I rode into the ring to collect his prize in a dream. The Union Jack was hoisted up the flagstaff, and the band played the National Anthem, unrehearsed, and in a minor key! I was presented with the lovely cup with the handles representing the Lions of Castile and supported by the bear—an emblem of Madrid.

On the national holiday of Corpus Christi, I was taken to Toledo to see the religious procession, and the fiesta bullfight. El Greco had lived in this capital of Old Spain, and painted some of his masterpieces in this ideal setting. Later that evening we were invited to an old monastery on a hill outside the town.

There was little twilight in the evening and darkness fell very quickly. From the terrace we could see the outline of Toledo, on its own hill, with the cathedral spire, the ruined fortress of the Alcazar, and the quaint old houses—silhouetted in the moonlight.

At the foot of the hill glistened the silver ribbon of the river. As we sat on the terrace steps some Spaniards produced their guitars and played flamenco music. There was the scent of roses in the still air and before long, everyone was singing folk songs. The moon passed over the sky, and I was under a spell of enchantment.

The spell broke when Prince Hal lamed himself on hitting just one fence at the Show. I did not realize then that he would be out of action for the whole summer until October. Another slight setback for me at Madrid was a bug called the Madrid tummy. I had thought that I was far too fit to pick up this tourist affliction. My mistake was made in drinking water from the tap when I was very thirsty one night. I had objected to paying more for a bottle of water than for a bottle of good local wine. The next morning I suffered the consequences and I staggered around feeling like death and only just managed to get to the Show to watch the finals of the World Championship. This was bound to be a most interesting competition with four finalists who finished in this order: Herr Winkler from Germany, M. Jonqueres d'Oriola from France, Captain Oppes from Italy and Comandante Gracia Cruz from Spain. There was an extra Spaniard in Senor Goyoaga who, a winner the year before, qualified to compete in the finals, and finished third between M. d'Oriola and Captain Oppes.

In the formula for the world championship, the finalists ride each horse in turn round the course. They jump their first round on their own horse. For the next rounds on their opponents' horses, they are allowed about two minutes to get used to each new horse. During this time they may jump two small fences that are placed in the ring, prior to starting their round. After they have ridden each horse, their total faults are added up. However, they are doubly penalized if they make a fault on their own horse.

Some of the riders had obviously watched the horses that they were going to ride, and studied the style and method in which they had been jumped. Then during the two minutes when they first rode each horse, they had to adapt themselves to suit the horse and apply the few hints that they had picked up.

It is an interesting competition from the spectators' point of view, when they can study the application of technique—I doubt if it can be good for the horses, who are already stars in their own right and used to one method and one rider.

I did not really concentrate much on the event as I was trying to stop myself fainting. I had not fainted since I was about seven years old, in church, and I staved it off until after the big event. Then I was supposed to receive the Grand Prix Cup, that Hal had won the day before, from Generalissimo Franco himself. Alas, I passed out just before the big moment, and before I was ushered through the cordon of his surrounding guards.

As I was swept away I could hear the microphone in the distance persistently calling for me.

I had the whole of the next day in which to recuperate before the evening performance for the Nations Cup. Even then, after spending most of the day in bed, I was not at my fittest for this last competition in Madrid. I was feeling very sorry for myself when a friend rang to ask if I would like to see the famous Alba collection of paintings. It was a chance that I could not miss, so I dragged myself up. Looking at these masterpieces made me feel so much better that I managed to change into my riding clothes. The evening performance eventually began at 11 p.m., for time is unimportant in Spain. It was 3.30 a.m. when the final national anthem was played. During the first round one of our team, Major Geoffrey Gibbon, broke a collar-bone in a fall, a disaster in a team event, and more than annoying for the sufferer.

By the time we were through with the transport and show arrangements, it was time for me to have some breakfast coffee before visiting my kind friends at Monasterio. I had been there during the 1951 visit to Spain, and the Duke of Pinohermoso had allowed me then to play a young fighting bull with a cape. Again this time, when we had driven across the plain that leads to the Guadarrama Mountains, we found the bulls and calves bred on the estate ready to test our bravery. The capes were produced, and after some of the polished performances given by the true matadors, we gave the toreros and the assembled company a little comic relief.

Yet more kindness was shown to me the following day, when a military car was provided to take two Spanish girl friends and myself to Segovia. I had planned an ambitious day which included seeing El Paular, the monastery hidden in the mountains, apart from seeing the great palace of San Ildefonso at La Granja before looking round Segovia. Our car must have divined my energetic programme—she started to boil anxiously while crossing the flat plain before the Guadarrama Mountains even came in sight. Places for water to quench her unassuagable thirst were few and far between. The driver was very philosophical about it, although he knew little of the workings of a car. Each time the car sang too loudly, we would stop and wait for the noise to subside. Then the radiator cap hardly needed a turn before a geyser of accumulated steam catapulted it across the road. There was no water on that mountain side, so when the cloud of steam had abated, the driver picked up the cap and screwed it on again. He shrugged his shoulders as he climbed into the driving seat—the car started. We found some water at a cottage further up the mountain. I think that the car was past caring, but it must have been just in time. While the radiator was being filled from a cup, the only available receptacle, a little donkey and her foal wandered up to see what we were doing.

With a great effort we managed to get over the Nevacerrada Pass, stopping at the ski club on top to celebrate our successful climb and refill the car. Finding the remote way to El Paular was out of the question by then, but we had no intention of turning back. The car regained her composure while we were coasting down the other side of the mountains, through peaceful and cool woods and glens. This part must be reminiscent of medieval England as the film of Robin Hood had been made in these surroundings. At last we arrived at La Granja. The Palace looked immense and sleepy in the sun. We managed to wake up an old man to take us to see some of the lovely Goya and Flemish tapestries. Our guide loved his tapestries and proudly led us down hall after hall giving the history of each of the vast works draping the walls. He would barely let us go in time to have a look at the enormous but now silent La Fama fountain, standing in the great gardens of the Palace. We had decided to lunch in Segovia, at Casa Candido under the great Roman aqueduct. This restaurant is famed for its roast sucking pig, a speciality of that province. There was no surprise when we arrived at about four o'clock for lunch, and never before have I had such delicious *cochonilla*. It dropped apart before the knife looked at it, and then the sucking pig melted in the mouth, before being washed down by local Segovian wine.

After such a meal we were well prepared to appreciate the charm of the old-world town. We wandered through narrow streets, and saw the cathedral with its priceless Rubens tapestries, and the Alcazar, the fortress of Segovia, built like a great ship on a high table of rock. Below us was the old 12th-century Church of the Knights Templar, Vera Cruz, standing alone with its dignity and age and ignoring the height and impressiveness of the Alcazar. That evening we drove back a less exciting way, under the silhouette of a mountain that looked like a woman at rest. Back in Madrid we retired to a roof garden, the guitars were produced and flamenco songs and music filled the still summer's night. I bought a guitar of my own the next day.

Before I left Madrid I had seen for the first time a rejoneador. This is the name for the man who rides his own superbly trained horses and fights the bulls from horseback as opposed to a matador who fights on his feet. I admired and was intrigued by the training of these fizzy little Andalusian horses for the dangerous work. A horse is naturally afraid of a bull, but these horses are trained to have such a degree of confidence in their rider that their obedience is complete, even when the bull is only a whisker away. They could perform difficult high school movements in front of the bull—then as the bull charged, he would find no horse where he expected to find contact with his horns. The horses had responded to the balance and judgment of the rider. Most of the time the rejoneador kept the reins hooked on to his belt, and did not need them for guidance. If a complete trust and sureness had not existed between the horse and rider, the bull would have found his target.

I was not particularly looking forward to the third show of the tour, held in central France at Vichy. I was loth to leave Spain; Prince Hal was lame; and after an all-night journey it was cold and wet in Vichy. I was longing to get home to get on with a lot of work that had accumulated there. To cap everything, the Madrid bug returned for two days, and riding was painful with a damaged rib and shoulder from a fall. I only had the one horse to jump. Eforegiot went extremely well, but somehow luck was not with us, and he just failed to win. The reward came on the last day, when I was determined that Eforegiot should win the Vichy Championship. He was in great form and jumped two unbeatable rounds, thus finishing off our tour in a spectacular fashion.

CHAPTER 14

PARIS AND BRUSSELS

I WAS thrilled to get home, but Tosca was fat and unfit
from her holiday. Prince Hal arrived back at Stroud
Station, and I went to meet him. I was certain that he
would be better, but my heart sank as we led him out
of the train box. He would hardly put his bad foot to
the ground, and the usual stiffness from a long journey
could not account for this. The White City, our most important international show, loomed ahead. I feared that
Tosca would not be fit in time, and now Prince Hal
looked a doubtful starter. The X-rays of Prince Hal's
foot did not show much, but after a most serious con-
sultation with Mr. J. R. Brain, our friend and vet for
the horses during the past two years, we came to a drastic
conclusion. Prince Hal had to have complete rest for at
least three months. I had had great hopes of competing
in Paris and Brussels during the autumn. Prince Hal
was at the height of his career and in his element
jumping indoors, but it was doubtful if he would
be right in time to get fit for these exacting competitions.

Tosca came to the White City with me, although she
had not had much work to prepare her. The first competition was the Selby Cup, which she had won twice
before. Luckily she really enjoys the White City, and

Pat Smythe

Flanagan and Prince Hal

in spite of not being fit she tried her best, and secured the lovely cup for the third time.

The honour of winning the Queen Elizabeth Cup has evaded me so far, and the next day we had this exciting contest. Tosca jumped faultlessly, and so did France's José Bonnaud on Charleston. In the jump-off on time Tosca nipped round the corners, and finished with a fast clear round. However, Charleston, last to go, galloped faster, and beat Tosca's time by a second. It was an exhilarating competition, and with the issue in the balance, it must have been exciting to watch.

Our National Championships were held at Blackpool, and again Tosca seemed to be in terrific form. But again we went from success to despair, as she developed some gland trouble on the last day and nearly died of internal poisoning. She took a long time to recuperate, and was still uncertain of herself by the time Harringay came round.

Before Tosca completely recovered, I went to Jersey for a day, and watched a horse show there. I was thrilled to find an enthusiastic and flourishing pony club on the island, in spite of the children having far less opportunity with the limited amount of land, and the difficulty of finding new ponies.

A week before Harringay, Prince Hal was allowed to start work. I did not think that he would be able to jump so soon. Tosca, too, was a doubtful starter. She had not really recovered her confidence after her illness, and I was afraid she would remember her fall at her last indoor show in America.

Horses have long memories, but luckily Tosca has happy ones of Harringay. It was a risk to take the two horses to Harringay, but this time it came off. Tosca won the B.S.J.A. Spurs again, and Hal, after winning the Diana Stakes, finished the show by winning the *Sunday Graphic* Cup, the Victor Ludorum Championship that Tosca had won the year before.

The rules for this championship ensure an exciting finish to the competition. The first round is jumped over a fairly big and long course. Then the jumps are altered to a test course with fewer and bigger fences. After the horses have jumped the second course, their faults for the two rounds are added together. This time there were five horse with no faults for jumping or time, so the fences were raised, and we jumped a third round. Our time counted on this final round if we were clear again. Miss Dawn Palethorpe jumped a fast clear round on Earlsrath Rambler, who had been going consistently well throughout the show. Then came Mr. Wilf White on Nizefella, and in this round he wasted no time. He made the last turn as he landed over the triple bar, galloped to the last fence, taking off at an almost impossible distance from the wall. He was clear, and the crowd waited tensely for his time to be announced. It was half a second slower than Earlsrath Rambler.

The crowd were still clapping the last horse as the bell rang for Prince Hal to start his round. I was over two fences, before I heard people quieten and settle to watch the horse now in the ring. Although one notices the crowd's noises and reactions, I was concentrating on cutting every possible second off the time of our round. Hal was in great form, but he was nearly too excited to turn quickly after the triple bar. I thought that we had a second or two in hand from a quicker turn after the

226

third fence—we galloped through the finish, I glanced up at the clock and saw that Prince Hal had won. What a compensation after the months of doubt, and the fears that he would not be able to jump again.

Tosca and Prince Hal left for Paris with Pauline two days before I joined them there. During the time after Harringay, they had had an easier time than I, but they were both fit, and in good form for the trip. Prince Hal especially had put on a lot of muscle with the three weeks of steady work. We were greeted in Paris with lovely weather. A further joy was to find the horses stabled in big comfortable boxes near to the Bois de Boulogne. Every other autumn we had competed at the indoor Paris show, the horses had not been stabled in luxury. Formerly, a storehouse had been converted into horse lines and the horses had to be tied up all the time. The horses usually developed coughs from the stuffy atmosphere, and they would not eat well. They could never rest peacefully with the noise of all the other horses, or lie down in comfort in their narrow stalls.

This had been the only place near the Vel d'Hiv, where the show was held, that could accommodate horses. With only a short time allotted in the morning for exercise in the small ring, it was difficult to give the horses enough work to prepare them for the evening performance. However, with the new arrangement and the comfortable boxes the horses were fit and happy. We could work them out of doors in the morning sun, and at night they were taken to the show. The articulated vans took six horses quite comfortably, although Tosca, being small, found the mangers a little high for her chin. The vans were built for racehorses like Prince Hal, so poor Tosca had to keep her head up while she was travelling.

On the first day of the show, I worked hard with both the horses in the morning. I have always found that they need to be extra obedient for the first competition, because they are more easily distracted by the strangeness of the surroundings. As they settle into the routine of jumping every evening, often with tiring jump-offs, so they need less work the following morning. Prince Hal is an exception to this, as he gets more and more energy the more work he has. So a great deal of surplus spirits have to be worked off every morning.

The first evening's jumping gave a good preview of the general standard for the show. The courses were big and yet all the horses jumped them well. There was plenty of excitement for the 15,000 spectators packed into the Vel d'Hiv. The crowd is always sympathetic and alive, most of them going there regularly to see any sport that is on, whether it be bicycle races, wrestling, boxing or the horse show.

Tosca was over-anxious and too careful in her competition, and lacked the necessary zip for the speed that counted on the first round. Prince Hal's class was for the horses that would be competing for the Grand Prix later in the week. The course was made up of combinations of fences with one or two strides between each. There were four horses with clear rounds, and for the jump-off the fences were raised. The time counted on this round, and Prince Hal was first to go. He was clear again, but the other riders had seen the pace that he had set. They were also without a fault and only four-fifths of a second divided all our times. Prince Hal was fourth. It is only a win that counts for international prestige, although there was so little between these four horses. During the round the rider cannot afford to relax from complete concentration for a fraction of a second. One hesitation or slight mistake puts one out of the running, and even a perfect round cannot win a timed competition unless it is carried out with speed and accuracy. The rider has to be prepared to take risks. It is an advantage to see the other horses jumping first, then one knows how many risks are necessary in order to beat their time.

The following evening, I nearly took one risk too many. It was at a time that mattered desperately as it was the first part of the Grand Prix. The twelve best horses qualified for the final of the Grand Prix, according to their results in three other competitions. This first part was a speed competition over quite big fences. I knew that the standard would be high, so if Prince Hal wanted a ribbon, we would have to do a fast clear round. Already some very good rounds had been jumped before my turn came. After jumping the first fence quite fast, I turned Hal quickly to save the distance before the next fence. It was not a difficult fence, but I had decided to jump it at an angle. Hal had sensed that this was a speed competition and was excited and unsettled. As we turned, he was fighting the bit, and did not see the fence until the last moment. His surprise made him stop—and so a small risk that should have come off resulted in a refusal which lost the competition. We finished the round without touching a fence, but three faults for the refusal put us sixteenth in the final placing.

I was most depressed about this, as we would have to

do extremely well in the other two competitions in order to get into the finals of the Grand Prix. In Paris, the only thing to do was to make the best of our unfortunate start. The next evening was free, so for the first time in my life I managed to get a seat for the Paris grand opera. The company were doing Weber's *Oberon,* with the ballet as well. The Opera House is an impressive sight, and every place was crammed before the curtain went up. With the opening scene, I found myself at the gates of fairyland. Two trees, standing like guardian dragons, showed the way to the gleaming white pinnacles of the fairy city. The ballet was like a dream and combined perfectly with the immense and beautifully dressed chorus. The splendours of the superb production reminded one of the extravagant days of Louis XV. After seeing the artistry of this performance and thinking of the work involved to produce such a fabulous combination of words, music and dancing, I went back to my job with renewed determination.

The next day Tosca was feeling herself on more familiar ground again. She was last to go in her speed class. The other competitors already knew their positions in the prize list, and Tosca had not shown enough form to worry them. However she did worry them when she scuttled round the fences, clear, and with the fastest time. The second part of the Grand Prix followed this and was again on time over a bigger course. This time I took no risks and Prince Hal was clear and placed fourth on time. I had one nasty moment when Hal thought he had to jump the left-hand of two fences placed side by side. We had taken off before I had persuaded him that our fence was on the right. He made an immense jump and cleared the right one. My heart was in my mouth, but we finished with a clear round.

This pulled us up a bit in the general placing, but our final position depended on the Puissance competition. On that evening the show was being televised for the English transmission. The B.B.C., used to our big international shows of Harringay and the White City with the split-second timing of the schedule and efficient military organization, had not realized that time is immaterial at foreign shows. Instead of giving the English public the thrilling finish to this Puissance competition, the people at home saw fences being moved, raised, lowered and moved again. Eventually before our television closed down, a few clear rounds had been jumped and so qualified for the jump-off but the most exciting part was yet to come.

The competition ended with a final jump-off over three huge fences. The first was a high wall with a bar beyond it. Voulette, a charming grey mare, the French hope, ridden by M. Jonquères d'Oriola, who had won the gold medal at Helsinki, just hit the bar by not spreading enough for this high and wide fence. Then the large parallel bars needed accurate jumping without losing the necessary impetus for such a spread. The last fence was the test, a dead straight wall standing well over 6 ft. with no marked ground line to make the horse jump it well. There had been no clear rounds over this final course when Prince Hal's turn came. He jumped the first two fences easily, but he was fighting with excitement when we turned for the wall. I thought that we were a little close on the take-off, but Prince Hal soared up and over to finish clear. Apart from the lovely deep blue Sèvres vase for this victory, he had ensured our place in the final twelve to jump for the Grand Prix.

By this time I knew that Prince Hal was in such fantastic form, that it would only be through a fault of mine if he did not fulfil my ambition for the year by winning the Paris Grand Prix. I felt my responsibility most terribly, and although one probably rides better when feeling calm and confident, I was tense and anxious. It is only too easy to get worked up about these jumping competitions. One is in the ring for about two minutes, and yet I frequently think over that round for the rest of the night. It is not only the winning round that is so exciting. Sometimes a horse produces a complete feeling of happy co-operation, and a joy of jumping. Although through some small fault he may not have won, the rider gets the utmost stimulation and excitement from the round. At one show, I was thrilled with a round that Tosca had jumped over a course that did not suit her. We had not won, but she had done everything I could wish for, and we had really enjoyed it. Somebody came up to me and said, "What is the matter with Tosca today?—not winning." Luckily horses are not machines.

On the night before the Grand Prix, the show did not finish until the early hours. We had had no supper, but I was ready for bed, in order to have as much sleep as possible before the big event. En route for the hotel, the others decided that they were too hungry so we called in at a bar in St. Germain des Prés. After having a sandwich, and joining in the dancing, there was little time left before I had to work the horses again. After riding in the Bois, I returned to the hotel at midday, where the draw for the order of jumping for the Grand Prix was to take place. The two prizes for the evening's competitions were being displayed at this official reception. I was certain that something would go wrong with my round for the Grand Prix, so I barely glanced at the superb cigar box that would be given to the winner. The prize that really attracted my attention was a lovely clock, with figures of little jumping horses round the dial. This could be won in Tosca's competition, and our dining-room at home so desperately needed a clock!

In the evening we had two reception parties before arriving at the show. I think that I was concentrating more on the evening performance ahead, than on social conversation around me. When we arrived at the Palais des Sports I went to see the horses. Paul was getting Tosca out of the van, ready for me to ride her into the ring. I was the first to go in the second section, so there was no hurry. After walking round the course, I was able to watch a few of the horses jumping in the first section. When I went to fetch Tosca we kept her as unexcited as possible. To warm her up, I trotted her down a side street, over the cobbles, away from the other horses. Then we were called into the ring. It was a touch and out competition with the horses jumping round the course until they made a fault. The winner had to jump the greatest number of fences in the time limit. Tosca was feeling in great form, and needed no winding up as she jumped fence after fence. Her time was nearly up, and she was very tired when I made a mistake and asked her to make too big an effort which finished our round. So far we were winning the competition, only there were still many more good horses to go. I could not wait to see the result of the other horses, as the Grand Prix followed immediately. Tosca was left in the collecting ring, and Paul took her saddle out for Prince Hal. I had to work him up and down a passage behind the Vel d'Hiv. He had been well drawn as eleventh to go out of the twelve horses. The only disadvantage being that he would be standing in the inside collecting ring, with no chance of moving until the other ten horses had jumped their rounds. Moreover the last of the twelve to go was the best of the French horses.

When Prince Hal had settled down outside, I rushed back to the arena, to see how Tosca's competition was faring. As I came through the door I heard a storm of clapping. This surely must be for a competitor that had beaten Tosca's time, or I thought that by then maybe she was out of the running. I tried not to appear too anxious as I asked people who was winning the competition. Nobody seemed to know. The competition was over, and I still did not know the results. The soldiers were already changing the course for the Grand Prix, when over the microphone the prizewinners were told to come into the ring immediately. Tosca had won by jumping two fences more than the others. I rushed excitedly to get her, only to find that she had no saddle. She was too hot from her exertion and the stuffy atmosphere for me to ride her bareback, so we managed to borrow a military saddle for her just in time to collect our prize. The dining-room at Miserden was going to get its clock.

Prince Hal was waiting at the arena entrance as I rode Tosca out. I leapt straight on to him, and into the ring for a quick canter before standing him in the inner collecting ring. Then only a moment was left for me to walk round the course, and size up the many problems for this all-important competition. Time was endless while the ten horses before me jumped their rounds. After seeing two or three times at least that Prince Hal's tack was correctly fitted, it was time to get on him. Once in the ring he settled down quickly, and he was jumping out of his skin over the fences. There was never a doubt about his clear round. Several of the other horses were also clear, and we all had to jump a second round. Again, the wait, the agony of watching before going into the ring again. I had been misinformed that the result of the Grand Prix was to be decided on the accumulation of faults and time on the two rounds. Prince Hal flashed round with another clear. His time was the fastest—but no, he had not won, the microphone informed us that two other horses that had also jumped two clear rounds would again jump off with Prince Hal, with the time counting only in this third round. All the strain again— the fences were raised, the air got hotter and dustier, the horses were sweating, and I felt worn out. It was getting on for midnight.

The first horse in was the Swedish Lurifax. Again he went clear, and up went the Swedish flag, but I knew that I could beat his time. I took no risks, and Prince Hal was clear again, almost wasting time in the air as he was clearing his fences by so much. His time was faster than the Swede's, so down came the Swedish flag, and up went the Union Jack. The last horse to go was Vezelise. He had jumped brilliantly for Captain Guy Lefrant throughout the show, and was the favourite for this prize. Vezelise jumped a fast round, but he was tired, and did not jump quite high enough. He finished with eight faults, and the Union Jack stayed in its place. Prince Hal came into the ring followed by Lurifax and Vezelise. The anthem was played and I felt like following it up with "Why, oh, why do I love Paris!"

I very nearly missed the train to Brussels. The horses were safely en route, but I tried to fit in more than was possible before leaving Paris. The traffic did all it could to hold us up on the way to the station, but by the time the train puffed out, I was on it.

The Palais des Sports in Brussels has a larger ring than Paris, although in both places there is a cycling track around the outside. The conditions were the same for the horses, and we worked them each morning in the woods outside Brussels, where they were stabled. In the evening they were transported to the show by huge vans, and before they came into the inner collecting ring we could give them a canter in a passage way.

Prince Hal was obviously in great form, and settled down to his jumping with sureness and enjoyment. Tosca was not so happy in the soft sand of the arena. Her feet sank into the sand, making it more difficult to jump, and she was ready for her winter's rest. Of the competitions, Prince Hal has never given me such a feeling of confidence as at this show. I had jumped at the show two years before, when Prince Hal and Tosca had won between them the Grand Prix de la Ville de Bruxelles. This had been a competition with the rider jumping the course with each of his two horses in turn, the winner having the least faults in the shortest time. Tosca and Hal rather specialize in this partnership type of competition, having won the President of Mexico Trophy in

New York, run on similar lines—so the horses had many friends in Brussels and people remembered them. One finds that any horse with a lot of character can make its personality felt with the crowd, sometimes even to the extent of getting fan mail and parcels of sugar!

It is always encouraging to a horse and the rider to have the crowd's enthusiasm. People are usually very fair, giving the greatest credit to the best performance, even if a foreign horse has beaten one of their own team. There are exceptions of course, just as the public at a bull-fight can turn against a matador. Then they force him into attempting the impossible, turning bravery into certain death. Too late, the people mourn the hero they have killed.

There was no hint of favouritism from the crowd when Prince Hal had his duel with Hicamboy—a Belgian horse. It was in the Puissance competition, when a reduced number of fences are greatly increased in size for each jump-off, until the winner is found. After the second jump-off, these were the only two horses clear, both good-looking chestnut geldings determined not to touch a fence. Hicamboy is a bigger horse than Prince Hal, but that was not to affect the issue. For the fourth round there were only two fences: first a straight red wall on the left-hand side of the arena, and then down the centre to an enormous spread fence, made of white bars either side of an imitation bank.

The Belgian horse ridden by M. Poffé went first. To the joy of the crowd he cleared both fences. Prince Hal came in. There was a hush from the crowd. He was pulling and fighting a little, as he still was not sure whether this round might be on speed—the possibility of a timed jump-off excited him terribly. I soon dispelled these thoughts of his by firmly keeping him in control at a slow canter before jumping the wall. In fact I had him almost too slow on the take-off, but in the last stride he crouched like a dog about to jump on to a high chair, and sprang over the wall with inches to spare. Turning for the spread fence, this control I had gained was more than necessary. There was the distraction of the "way out" after the big jump; the gates into the collecting ring opened in a direct line after the fence. All horses are keener on the homeward journey, and these gates were an enticement. However, we were under control as we cantered down and jumped the fence to qualify for the next jump-off. Up went the two fences, the spread was widened, and men were running about getting new layers to put on the wall. Into the ring went Hicamboy. He scraped over the wall, but it did not fall, and when he cleared the spread, in grand style, the crowd went mad. Prince Hal stumbled in the soft sand churned up at the corner of the ring, as I turned him for the wall, but as we approached he had settled, and was well balanced. After jumping it I turned for the last fence, and had the luck to sense the correct stride for the take-off as we turned. It could not have been easier. For the sixth round, it did not look so easy. The wall was up to 6 ft. 6 ins. and so was the last fence, which also added the problem of a 6 ft. 6 ins. spread. The jumps were high, the hour was late, and the horses were hot.

The battle was on, and Hicamboy faced the wall yet again. He cleared it, and there was a "shush" from some people to stop the crowd clapping in jubilation before he jumped the last fence. Alas, he could not manage the huge spread and he hit it badly. Hal was keen to get going, and there was a murmur from the crowd as if they were speculating on his chances. He jumped the wall, and turned nearly too quickly. For a moment he seemed too excited to be obedient, and it would be a very nasty moment for the rider if he arrived inaccurately at a fence of this size. Hal's courage was superb, and he used all his ability to gather himself, and easily cleared the spread. I felt as though we were diving down from the stars as we landed on the sand as winners of the Puissance.

The final competition was a high jump in place of the usual Grand Prix. Prince Hal was entered for this although he had never before competed in a competition of this type. Each horse is allowed three tries to clear the high jump before qualifying for the next height. The first time, with the fence at about 5 ft. 6 ins., Hal was surprised to find that he only had one obstacle to tackle. He soon got the idea, and each time the fence went up he jumped it on his first try. By the time we reached 6 ft. 6 ins. we were getting a little anxious as to whether the poles would last out for a further height. The poles are specially made of padded bamboo, so that the horses will not damage themselves. So many poles had been broken by horses that could not quite make the height, that the carpenters had to start a running repair service.

There were only three horses left to face 2 m. 10 (6 ft. 10⅞ ins.) and when Prince Hal jumped it I was thrilled. Col. Llewellyn's great horse Kilgeddin had cleared that height with me in Paris. It was the first time since that night in 1950 that I had competed in another high jump.

At 2 m. 20 (7 ft. 3 ins.) Prince Hal again jumped it

on his first attempt. He had won the competition, so there was no need to ask more of him. He also now held the official Ladies' European High Jump record. He was the leading horse of the show, and with the points also gained by Tosca, he made me the leading rider of the show. Prince Hal deserved a crown. The greatest credit was also due to Pauline for keeping the horses so well through the strenuous shows, long journeys and hours of waiting in winter weather.

When the horses arrived back at Miserden they found the flags out and "Welcome" over their stable door. The rain was dripping off the Union Jack outside, but there was a good feed in the manger inside the stable. They were worn out after their journey home, and retired to bed soon after they had eaten their supper. The next morning Prince Hal refused to get up, but condescended to eat his feed off the floor while he was lying down. He demanded the least privilege of a hero—breakfast in bed.

During the winter the horses are rested. On fine days they are allowed out in the paddock, where they give a rodeo display of bucking, to show the joy of living. They look so bonny and feel so naughty that I always fear that their sense of humour will be worked off on me when we start work again.

After the high lights of the shows, the star performers become bored with their temporary retirement: but this is the time when their legs can be rested, and they can forget the strain of the big competitions. They then come back to their work with renewed zest at the beginning of the next season.

The rider has no such rest. I can use this time to concentrate on finding and training young horses ready to start in novice jumping events in the spring. One cannot produce a top-class horse in a moment, and it is the hours of background work put in at home that count in the long run. Years later, one hopes to get the thrill and satisfaction from having the horse that has been trained at home, winning and jumping consistently. On the other hand, after all this work, one may find that the horse lacks some quality to make him a top-class performer. Then with patience, one must start training another, with faith that the result will prove more satisfactory. Life is never dull, for the more horses I ride, the more I learn how little I know. Success in any walk of life is never easily won, but in show jumping, the work behind the scenes is always interesting and worth while.

CHAPTER 15

MUSEUM PIECE

No ONE knows my Cotswold village of Miserden who does not know Miss Timms, the blacksmith's daughter.

Miss Timms, the petrol pump proprietor and maker of fine wines—the robust, homely, resolute Miss Timms, who comes down the hill like a ship in full sail.

High on the list of my favourite villagers, she is a woman of action among the one hundred and fifty souls of Miserden community; a leader of the Women's Institute and of most other pursuits of good citizenship; the church organist with a liking for volume and vigour to go with the melody. Decades ago her father was the craftsman blacksmith of the village, and when he died his daughter ran the smithy, aided by the traditionally iron biceps of Mr. Roseblade. From the days when Mother and I were at Birdlip and Crickley, and again when we came to Miserden, the shoeing of all our horses was arranged and supervised by Miss Timms—until 1954, when the sad blow of Mr. Roseblade's death brought the smithy to an end and sent us to Cirencester for our shoeing. Often I had gone into the small parlour behind the shop to sit with Miss Timms, sampling her delicate creations of cowslip, elderberry, and sloe wines, or a home-made liqueur.

One spring evening, I met her in the lane, and was

about to describe for her some impressive American recipes: a delicious egg-nog with a bottle of rum, seven beaten eggs, milk, thick cream, and a half-pound of icing sugar; or the potent concoction of brandy, rum, eggs, hot water, and nutmeg which I had consumed before a Mississippi snack that included lobster tails and *crème de menthe frappée*.

But Miss Timms gave me a wave of greeting and spoke first.

"I've made a new potato wine—you must come and try it," she said; and suddenly my exciting brews of rum and brandy, eggs and nutmeg, seemed merely pretentious. There was something mighty in the thought of Miss Timms' potato wine; it restored a certain humility and my sense of values.

At home, in and about the Dower House, something of the spirit of my mother remains: her infectious fun and gaiety, a hint of the impromptu, and, when the house is full of guests, warmth of friendliness, the easy relations of live and let live; these I regard essentially as qualities that Mother left behind. She also began a theme that grows stronger year by year, the international nature of my Cotswold guest house. The children of parents living abroad, along with children from foreign countries; sometimes a girl from France, a lad from Switzerland, a family from Sweden, Germany, Holland, Belgium, Spain, Ireland, Australia, New Zealand, the United States. Some ride, some lounge in deck-chairs, some come to watch show jumping, some to hear Shakespeare at Stratford; some play tennis, or hockey on the lawn with walking sticks. All are enchanted with the Cotswold countryside.

At one time I added the guest-house cooking to my already overcrowded days, but soon the burden became too heavy, and nowadays it is shouldered by my housekeeper; the only other member of our whole-time Miserden kitchen force is Wilf, the lean, happy, obliging, elderly kitchen boy; and, of course, there's the invaluable Mrs. Winter, our daily help. For me, the guests, the horses, the endless accounts, the correspondence, the organization of shows and the shopping have been greatly eased by the recent arrival of an invaluable friend, Paddy Bury. There never seems to be much time for sleep, but luckily I manage without a great deal.

Outside the Dower House, Pauline, my groom, finds a firm satisfaction in the responsibilities of the stables. Paul is my companion around the shows; often we both sleep in the horsebox and take turns at the primitive cooking facilities.

Converting the box (usually at agricultural shows) into living quarters involves a lengthy chore. When the horses are disposed of we first muck out the box and air it a little, then push the hay bales to one end, find a corner for the oats, bran, and chaff, hang up the bridles and saddles, lay a couple of blankets, bring in our pyjamas and suitcases and settle for the night—I in Tosca's section, Paul in Prince Hal's. It saves hotel bills. One night I had gone to a show ball, and returned long after midnight to find Paul asleep; quietly I took off my evening dress, shoes, and stockings, folded them away, then became furious at the discovery that I had dropped an ear-ring—presumably in the straw of my horsebox cubicle. I searched for forty minutes without success; next morning I told Paul of the loss and we renewed the search. I examined almost every handful of straw we possessed, but the ear-ring was nowhere to be found. Six weeks later I discovered my piece of jewellery—in the turn-up of a pair of old corduroys which had been hanging on the horsebox wall that night.

With a fierce devotion, Pauline defends Prince Hal against every criticism, especially when it comes from show-jumping people who consider that an excitable thoroughbred is the "wrong type" for the ring. She was politely glad when Tosca became the Leading Horse in Great Britain, yet I know that she was far more pleased about Hal's third place among the nation's show jumpers. There can be no denying that Hal is excitable; he is also ticklish, especially when being groomed, and has a tendency to bite. As might be expected, Pauline gets bitten more than anyone else, although even Colonel Harry Llewellyn has had cause to jump hurriedly out of Hal's way. In reply, Harry gave Prince Hal the defamatory title "Vampire", and when he later presented us with two nameplates for the horses, he inscribed upon Prince Hal's the malevolent instruction: "Feed This Horse on Fresh Blood." Pauline was white with anger.

Not that Pauline's enthusiasm for Hal ever produces neglect of Tosca, who appears at big shows as beautifully groomed—with her mane and tail well washed—as the handsome Hal. With Paul it is always the horses first, herself last, and when we are abroad her efforts to turn them out in tip-top condition call forth the plaudits of both friends and rivals. For a girl of her stature she has a prodigious strength, which astonished the grooms and attendants in New York during our 1953 international tour. A gang of men were unloading enormous metal trunks, each weighing two to three hundredweight, containing the horses' tackle. Paul grasped one end of a trunk while a burly New York porter, at the other side, gave a patronizing grin, saying:

"Now don't be ridiculous, honey—you know you can't handle the big stuff."

Pauline said nothing, but without a stagger pulled the trunk across the ground, while the "tough guy", almost on his knees at the other end, made a weakly effort to assist.

In a different context, I too go down on my knees—to the horses, whose courage and brilliance have taken me already into a dozen foreign countries and a thousand new experiences. But show jumping has brought much more than a broadminded outlook and the opportunity to travel. It has, I believe, improved my capacity for concentration, not only in the arena but in all of modern life's activities; it has given me confidence and an awareness of the pitfalls of too much confidence; it has eradicated any desire to show off, for I have learned that my best-loved horse may take it into his head to dump me from the highest peaks of success into the bottom of a fence; it has fostered the powers of quick thinking, slow patience, accurate judgment, and good co-ordination; and, above all, it has taught me that show jumping itself need not be the sole object of human effort and existence. Indeed, it is not my intention to die an old maid—not even gloriously—in the middle of an international show ring. On the other hand, I have an equally strong resistance to rushing the fences of marriage, despite five dashing proposals uttered, so far, in four languages. When I marry, I shall hope to be entering a relationship more vital to me than anything gone before. I want therefore to approach it thoughtfully, to adapt myself, and to make it last; and if it seems likely that those successes will be achieved, then the arenas of show jumping may become considerably less important to me. This notion badly fits the annoying newspaper story of a certain "interview" with me, but that is hardly my fault. I was once reported ("I asked Miss Smythe what her ambition was") as saying: "I want to go on and on, winning until I am the best in the world." I shuddered as much for the crudity of the style as for the total inaccuracy of the boast.

While they last, nevertheless, the contests of the ring will continue to be a tonic. The best part of jumping is the sheer exhilaration of it and I love it. Of course I also enjoy winning, especially a really difficult competition, and I cannot help remembering that I need to win in order to balance the budget. Abroad, we sometimes get prizes like Hal's lovely rug, which has proved more useful than my cigar box for the Prix du Champion!

There are, of course, compensations in the nagging necessity for having to budget carefully. I have learned, for example, how to ferret out good clothes at reasonable prices in the most unlikely places. Luckily, I can be fitted off the peg, and rarely pay more than ten guineas for a suit (often with two skirts). Two of my best autumn outfits at this price level came from a small shop in one of the lesser industrial towns of the Midlands—a coat and a suit, admired if not envied by some of my wealthier American acquaintances. I am also a January Sales "browser", around the middle rather than the first of the bargain-hunting days, and here, too, a sharp eye or a lucky strike have won me some first-rate dresses and accessories, including a short evening wrap and several handbags. Show jumping *could*, if I let it, turn my clothes bills into major burdens, for apart from costly riding garments, and all that goes with them, I need an enormous variety of reasonably smart outfits for the social as well as the working life of international competitions; it is neither possible nor desirable to attend an official party in a gingham frock; and I would not enjoy making a trip to the B.B.C., even between events, wearing my riding things. For international shows abroad, clothes must look to the climate, and on journeys to France or Belgium I have had to pack cocktail dresses, ballet-length evening frocks, and suits, to cope with functions ranging from the informal sherry party to the night-time banquet, along with morning receptions, formal luncheons, afternoon receptions, and visits to the opera.

Two of the most intriguing events of this social scene took place in London. The first was a meeting I had thought about ever since my wartime schooldays, and it happened in no less imposing a household than that of the Chancellor of the Exchequer, at 11 Downing Street, where Ronald took me to a literary cocktail party. Here I came face to face with my hero-in-chief among actors, Sir Laurence Olivier, whose performance as King Henry V had inspired the renaming of Fourtowns, my chestnut thoroughbred, who became . . . Prince Hal. Keeping the adolescent promise I had made myself, I told the story to Sir Laurence; he was mildly interested, but as he listened I realized I was telling it all with a casual matter-of-factness in place of the tense excitement I had coyly imagined long ago. The change, I decided, was merely that I had grown up.

The second memorable occasion was an evening in 1953 when the White City international show had ended. The Duke and Duchess of Beaufort, whom I knew well, for I had hunted often with the Beaufort hounds of which the Duke is Master, were giving an informal party at Kensington Palace. Among the guests was Princess Margaret, who had watched the show jumping that night, and had, I learned, kindly said she wished to see me.

After a hot bath at a friend's flat I put on an evening dress, got into my van, and hurried to the Palace. Hurried for two reasons—first, I did not want to be late; secondly, I felt famished after a hectic day's jumping and an inadequate lunch. I was delighted, therefore, when I saw that a buffet supper was arranged under the gleaming chandeliers.

Over drinks, I talked with Princess Margaret, who had found the evening's contest highly exciting to watch, and I observed the truth of what I had so often heard; Princess Margaret, like her sister, the Queen, knew what she was talking about where horses were concerned. At White City that night, in the test competition, I had ridden Colonel Llewellyn's Lady Jane, a fine mare who had never before jumped in an important test event; it was also the first time I had ever sat on her back. The Princess knew that Lady Jane had jumped over six feet, beating some of the best French horses in the process, but was impressed to learn that this was my first ride with the mare; she then demanded details of how I fared, and went on to question me closely about the kind of life I led travelling to show after show. A most interesting encounter, and a stimulating party.

Not even Princess Margaret, of course, can rival the Queen in her knowledge of horses. The Duke told me that often, sitting with the Queen at a show, he would begin explaining helpfully: "This, by the way, is such-and-such a horse." The Queen would nod and comment: "Yes, I know—he's by the stallion So-and-so." No other Queen of England has understood horses better, nor ridden so well.

When I returned from America early in 1954, several agreeable tasks awaited me. One was a B.B.C. recorded programme for the series "Frankly Speaking", in which I was questioned for half an hour about my life and interests by a trio that included the great Roger Bannister, who was soon to shatter that barrier of the athletic stratosphere, the four-minute mile. Then came a request for my signature that had me sitting half the night at my Miserden dining-table surrounded by thick, thin, fountain, mapping, and ball-point pens with which to write my own name on a hundred and one sheets of scrap paper. Eventually, and a little shamefaced, I produced an autograph which looked clean, clear, and dignified, placed it in an envelope and walked with it to the pillar box at 4 a.m. This signature was a specimen to be used in the inscription for a finely-made glass tankard designed for presentation to Queen Elizabeth. The message on it said:

"*Further jewels for Her Majesty's crown, contributed during the first year of her reign by these her loyal subjects. . . .*"

Then followed the signatures of Sir John Hunt, Len Hutton, Gordon Pirie, Neville Duke, Mike Lithgow—and me. As I dropped the envelope in the box, I did not feel like a jewel.

Until the summer of 1954 I had not paid a visit to the celebrated waxworks of Madame Tussaud since childhood. The acquaintance was renewed by a letter, from Mr. Tussaud, informing me that they would be glad to "do" me—in wax. I accepted the honour, drove to London, and went to Baker Street for the preliminaries. Before they were through with my limbs and expressions it had turned into one of the most absorbing experiences of a lifetime, with Mr. Tussaud, Mr. Edds, his colleague, and a small company of highly-skilled technicians giving an immense amount of detailed study to all my features which was almost embarrassing.

First they photographed my face from every possible angle, including the worst ones. Then they matched my hair and invited me to watch how they performed the process of "growing" hair upon the waxen head. This was expertly done by a girl with the patience of Job; one by one, every strand is fixed to the head, a labour lasting a fortnight. I watched, fascinated, while the operation went on, and as the wax face turned slowly towards me I recognized the unmistakable features of Sir Winston Churchill.

"But surely Churchill has been in Madame Tussaud's since before I was born?" I said, puzzled. They smiled, and reminded me of the notorious intruder who had shattered, temporarily, the Premier's waxworks personality. This was the *new* Churchill head.

A week later I returned to the Tussaud museum to give

them my eyes. The German technician in charge showed me the slightly macabre but entrancing creation of wax figure eyes, glass pellets of blindness which he made by melting small sticks of different coloured quartzes in the flame of a blowlamp. The mixture of quartzes is designed to match the eye texture and colours of the subject. Each eyeball is measured, and shaped with a lovely precision; then come the frills. I watched the minute veins painted into the whites of my eyes and learned from the German technician that in my iris, the dark outer rim which enclosed an inside rim of a deeper brown was unusually difficult to achieve. I made a mental note to pay particular attention, whenever I might see the finished product, to my dark, difficult, and obviously unique outer rim.

Then they got my hands; an hour and a half was passed, in wax, by each hand. And finally, they took—or at any rate they wanted—the clothes from my back; coat, hat, breeches, even my riding boots. It was, they said, an unswerving tradition to use only the genuine personal garments of the man or woman portrayed.

"What about Crippen? And Hitler?" I asked with some surprise, for their clothes cannot have been available. But the question was ignored. I sent the clothes along, all the same. The honour of appearing on the Tussaud stage was not to be sneezed at.

A few days later I began booking ship passages for Prince Hal and Eforegiot and a plane seat for myself, in preparation for our international shows in Portugal and Spain during June 1954. I saw no more of my waxwork figure, but the thought of it was pleasing and very novel —as if, I told myself, you are leaving something of yourself in old England while you jump and go gallivanting in foreign parts. I knew, too, that my silent wax self would be sitting on a wall not far away from the figure of a horseman without whose brilliance, patience, devotion, and courage there would be no British show jumping team worthy of the name, no international battles for us to fight, no trophies to tell the story of fair triumphs, no tours abroad for young women such as me—and certainly no waxwork show jumpers. Colonel Harry Llewellyn.

As a non-starter in the political arena, I would not dare to be dogmatic about a certain nice point of speculation which from time to time runs through my mind. How (I wonder) would the infant struggle of British international show jumping have fared were it not for the political upheaval of 1945 which brought a Socialist government into power? A far-fetched question, no doubt. Or is it?

In the post-war years, the strong, energetic, Welsh Colonel called Harry Llewellyn was one of Britain's coal owners, the head of a colliery which he had successfully built up to maximum production.

Then, in 1947, the nation's pits were nationalized, and the owners bought out. One result of this was that Harry Llewellyn lost interest in collieries. Instead, he threw his vast energies wholly into this other enthusiasm— show jumping competitions—where he already possessed a considerable name. And within two years of nationalization, Harry Llewellyn's bold, single-minded devotion to the cause of building a British team had changed the open mockery of Continental riders to a ready acknowledgment of our competence.

It is possible, even probable, that British jumping would have improved through the years if Harry Llewellyn had stayed in his managing director's chair. It is certain, however, that it could never have soared so far, so quickly. Indeed, it was the impact of political events that gave him the initiative to concentrate on this sport that has grown from fox-hunting. His horses gained valuable experience abroad and Foxhunter became world famous. With Colonel Ansell working behind the scenes to produce a better team, Britain progressed from an Olympic bronze medal in 1948 to a gold medal by 1952. It will be interesting to see if there are any ladies in the 1956 Olympic teams, now that the rule has been changed to allow them to compete.

My own experience of Harry runs on two levels: I know him as a masterly exponent of show jumping, stern, silent, and determined in the arena; and as a good-natured friend with unbounded energy, a quick wit, a character full of fun, and a brilliant talker at all times. Teeny Llewellyn, his wife, has been a heaven-sent companion on some of our tours, since only with her have I been able to discuss the thousand and one topics and problems which the men of any team find merely tiresome. Not that Harry and other male show jumpers are ungallant. In Paris one night we all went to hear *Madame Butterfly*. Another night to hear *Aïda*. Harry heard a good deal of both; at one theatre he dozed off for less than five minutes, but really thoroughly enjoyed the performance. Back in London, I telephoned Teeny and told her of our theatre visits. She said:

"What! You got Harry to hear opera?"

"Yes, of course," I answered.

254

"Harry to the opera! Are you talking about *my husband*? At the opera . . . ?" And Teeny dissolved into helpless laughter. Thus do we treat the master of British show jumping.

I have had one further point of association with the family of Colonel Llewellyn. Some years ago I made the tragic mistake of becoming engaged to Harry's son, David. I remained his fiancée until 1953, when the blow fell.

Without warning, without pity, David broke the silence one summer afternoon.

"I've got another fiancée now; you're too old."

David will be ten next birthday.

Harry to the opera? Are you taking about me, madam? At the opera ...?' And I was dragged into helpless laughter. Thus do we meet the master of ninety- show-jumping.

I have left out further plant of our labors with two chunks of Colonel Llewellyn. Suffice it to say that I man- ... trick or so of ... to Harry's son David. I remained his fiancée until ... when the table fell.

Without warning. Without pity. David broke the silence one summer afternoon.

'It's got another kitten now! You're too old.'

David will be ten next birthday...